GREAT
CHRISTIAN
BOOKS

GREAT
CHRISTIAN
BOOKS

by

HUGH MARTIN

Essay Index Reprint Series

 BOOKS FOR LIBRARIES PRESS
FREEPORT, NEW YORK

INTERNATIONAL STANDARD BOOK NUMBER:
0-8369-2242-5

LIBRARY OF CONGRESS CATALOG CARD NUMBER:
71-142666

PRINTED IN THE UNITED STATES OF AMERICA

CONTENTS

ILLUSTRATIONS
(Facsimile)

I

The Power of the Book

" WHAT would become of our world if some new disease
were suddenly to attack paper, and reduce all our libraries
to dust? " That is the question put to us by a modern
French writer, Duhamel, in his book *In Defence of Letters*.
He answers it by declaring, " I believe that if humanity
were to lose its libraries, not only would it be deprived of
certain treasures of art, certain spiritual riches, but more
important still, it would lose its recipes for living "—by
which he means the fruit of accumulated experience of how
to do things, whether it be making puddings or building
ocean liners. None of us could contemplate without con-
sternation a world without books. All modern culture is
bound up with the printed page. H. G. Wells in his *Outline
of History* shows how the invention of paper liberated the
human mind and made possible the spread of knowledge.
It is difficult to realize that the discovery of movable type,
which has so revolutionized life, is only five centuries old.
Of course there were books before then, but they were rare
and costly, and accessible only to the few.

The influence of books can scarcely be exaggerated. In
the long run the writer is more powerful than the soldier;
it is the thinker who recruits and moves the army. Perhaps
the most influential figure in the last two hundred years
was not Napoleon, but the German philosopher, Hegel. He
is the real father of modern nationalism and so of Fascism
and Nazism; and by a curious paradox he is at the same
time the father of Communism.

In *Nationalism: Man's Other Religion* Edward Shillito
pictured three readers in the British Museum some seventy
years ago poking fun over their sandwich lunch at another
reader—" a German, perhaps, with more than a touch of
Jerusalem "—who sat day by day reading Hegel and writing

9

innumerable notes. They laugh at this dreamer and spinner
of cobwebs. "It's a good thing," says one of them, "that
there are men of action about, men who do things. . . ."
The name of the poverty-stricken spinner of cobwebs was
Karl Marx. His cobwebs proved highly explosive. His
brooding and study in Soho and the Museum Reading
Room have shaken the world.

But this general question of the power of books in the
life of the world, fascinating as it is, would lead us far
beyond the possible limits of this volume, which is concerned only with the place of books in the Christian faith.
That itself is a vast subject, and all that one man or one
book can do is to illustrate it by a choice of examples.

The Bible, of course, stands in a place by itself. No
human pen could trace more than the merest outline of
its power over man, or tell the tale of those whose lives
have been transformed by the reading of it—from, say,
Augustine obeying the command to "take up and read"
to Tokichi Ishii, the Japanese murderer, converted only a
few years ago by reading the New Testament left in his cell
by a missionary, picking it up out of sheer boredom, just to
pass the time. Now his own autobiography, *A Gentleman
in Prison*, goes all over the world, in its own humble turn
calling men to Christ, as does the immortal autobiography
of Augustine.

There is an apostolic succession of Christian books trace-
able from the New Testament onwards. St. Augustine was
kindled by St. Paul. Dante found inspiration in Augustine
and Bernard, as well as in the classics of Greece and Rome.
Petrarch wrote of Augustine: "Whenever I read your *Confessions* . . . I seem to be reading the history of my own
wanderings and not of another's." So Saint Teresa also
declared that she saw herself described in the *Confessions*.
"When I came to the conversion," she adds, "and read
how he heard that voice in the garden, it seemed to me
nothing less than that one had uttered it for me. I felt it
so in my heart."[1] Luther set the Bible and the *Confessions*

[1] *Autobiography*, ix. 9.

above all other books. John Bunyan found in Luther's commentary on the Galatians, his own condition "so largely and profoundly handled as if his book had been written out of my heart. . . . I do prefer this book of Martin Luther upon the Galatians (excepting the Holy Bible) before all the books that ever I have seen, as most fit for a wounded conscience."[1] And one could easily write a book about the influence of John Bunyan's own writings upon men of many lands.

Indeed the tale is endless, and we must not attempt to carry it further here, though later pages have more to say of the far-reaching influence of the books of Augustine and William Law, for example.[2] Thomas à Kempis, himself among the great succession, has a true word to say on this theme: "If he shall not lose his reward who gives a cup of cold water to his thirsty neighbour, what will not be the reward of those who by putting good books into the hands of those neighbours, open to them the fountains of eternal life?"

During the past twelve months I have taken down from my shelves an armful of books that have spoken home to me at various times of my life. I have re-read them and tried to set down in writing the essence of their message—for me at any rate. By doing this I hope to induce others to read—or re-read—the books for themselves. Perhaps what I have written may be a guide in understanding them, though I make no pretence of having engaged in any profound research or of having said anything that will be new to students of these men. So far as I could, I have tried to let them speak for themselves. I have not sought to elaborate the lessons that I see in them for modern man or for the modern world, but that the lessons are there I have no doubt at all, and they will be found by those who read them.

These are all living books that have spoken to many thousands besides me, yet perhaps nobody else would have

[1] *Grace Abounding*, 129-30.
[2] See pp. 16, 81.

made this precise selection. At any rate I made it first of all for personal reasons. Many other books on my shelves had an almost equal claim upon me: John Woolman, John Wesley, Lancelot Andrewes, Richard Baxter very nearly joined the company. And others might have followed: "the river of God is full of water." But in the end these seven seemed to choose themselves.

Now that they are spread out before me I am interested to note their variety and how they span the Christian centuries from the fourth down to yesterday. They are African, Scottish, French and English; Catholic Bishop, Covenanter, monk, Puritan parson, Non-Juror, Baptist missionary, poet of Independent stock. What a fascinating company they would make if they could be gathered together in a room.

St. John the Divine tells us that there are twelve gates to the City of God. These men used seven of them. How impoverished we are if we set ourselves down beside the gate by which we entered, with no eyes for the company that presses in on every side. There are some poor souls who speak as if they would like to close the other eleven gates, or even, ludicrously enough, to deny that the other entrances exist at all. Here, even in these seven, is glorious variety.

Yet it is hard to say if their unity is not even more impressive than their variety. For all their differences these men preach one Lord, one Faith. "All these worketh that one and the self-same Spirit, dividing to every man severally as He will" (1 Corinthians xii. 11). One of the things that made the early Christians catch their breath in wonder was that God created a true unity out of Greek and Jew, barbarian, Scythian, slave and free (Colossians iii. 11). Again and again the New Testament returns to the theme. We of this generation have much more cause to wonder and to rejoice, as we can see how Christ has met the needs of men of every land. Certainly no one who reads the books discussed here can fail to be impressed by the fundamental unity of their message.

This consensus of the saints is surely a powerful argument for the objective reality behind their common faith. For these men are not repeating what they have read in a book or echoing what somebody told them. They have found out for themselves. Separated by many centuries, of very diverse temperaments, with different degrees of cultural attainment, and of widely varied ecclesiastical traditions, these men who have explored far along the Christian road bring back substantially the same report as to what they have seen.

Dean Inge emphasizes this fact in summing up his book on *Christian Mysticism* (p. 325). "These men of acknowledged and pre-eminent saintliness agree very closely in what they tell us about God. They tell us that they have arrived gradually at an unshakable conviction, not based on inference, but on immediate experience, that God is a Spirit with whom the human spirit can hold intercourse; that in Him meet all that they can imagine of goodness, truth and beauty; that they can see His footprints everywhere in nature, and feel His presence within them as the very life of their life, so that in proportion as they come to themselves, they come to Him. They tell us that what separates us from Him and from happiness is first, self-seeking in all its forms, and secondly, sensuality in all its forms; that these are the ways of darkness and death, which hide from us the face of God; while the path of the just is like a shining light, which shineth more and more unto the perfect day. As they have toiled up the narrow way, the Spirit has spoken to them of Christ, and has enlightened the eyes of their understandings, till they have at least *begun* to know the love of Christ which passeth knowledge and to be filled with all the fulness of God."

Christian experience is more extensive and more manifold than these seven books reveal. There are aspects of Christian discipleship which are particularly important in our generation about which they seem to have nothing to say. Indeed some readers may approach this book with the feeling that it is rather remote and irrelevant, even that it represents an unworthy kind of "escapism" at such an hour as this.

As to that, several comments might be made. For one thing, these men, even if it may not be immediately apparent in the particular writings studied here, were nearly all very much concerned with the social and political problems of their own generations. St. Augustine, as will be pointed out, lived at a time of testing as stern as our own, when a whole civilization was collapsing, and his work did much to guide the task of "reconstruction." Samuel Rutherfurd, John Bunyan and William Law all endured persecution for their faith. Rutherfurd confronted a totalitarian state in defence of "the crown rights of Christ in His Church." Bunyan fought in the Civil War as well as contending for religious liberty in the preaching of the Gospel. Law gave up everything for conscience' sake. William Carey was a staunch opponent of the slave trade and laboured through a long life for the social welfare of the Indian peoples. These men were not all of one mind politically or socially, and we need not necessarily agree with any of them to realize that they had at least no circumscribed view of the implications of the Christian faith in the social setting of their day. They were no "escapists" whatever else may be said of them.

But we must go on to recognize that it may be precisely in what is unfamiliar or even uncongenial in these seven books that much of their value for us may lie. Some of our modern emphases in Christian thinking may need correction. We must be ready to listen to these men as well as to criticize them.

These books are for the most part concerned with God's intimate dealings with the human soul. They deal with sin and salvation, with God's call and man's response. They bring us back to the heart of things. It is entirely right that we should be deeply concerned for social justice and security, for the creation of a stable international order, for the reconstruction of a shattered society. But men themselves need reconstructing before they can do much to reconstruct society. It is because we are not in right relations with God that the secret of true human relationships evades us.

William Temple closed his book on *Christianity and Social Order* with these words: "I should give a false impression of my own convictions if I did not here add that there is no hope of establishing a more Christian social order except through the labour and sacrifice of those in whom the Spirit of Christ is active, and that the first necessity for progress is more and better Christians taking full responsibility as citizens for the political, social and economic system under which they and their fellows live."

I believe that these masters of the spiritual life in their different ways can help us to be better Christians and inspire us to accept our own responsibility as citizens in our own generation.

II

The Confessions of St. Augustine
(354-430)

Few men have made so deep a mark on history as Augustine, Bishop of Hippo. Those who have a right to offer such an estimate have often named him as the greatest Christian thinker next to the Apostle Paul. Harnack, for example, says that he is incomparably the greatest Christian " between Paul the Apostle and Luther the Reformer."[1] Vernon Bartlet says that " he has left a profounder impress upon the human soul in the Western world than any other since the Christian era, save the Apostle Paul."[2] No subsequent Christian thinker could ignore his work. His name is inevitably in the index of nearly every theological work of weight throughout the centuries right up to the present day.

Describing Augustine as "the greatest of all Western thinkers," Gwatkin sums up the wide range of his influence in striking words. "One part of his capacious mind fixed the ruling ideas of the Middle Ages, while another set the problems of the Reformation. He is the father of Catholicism and also of Protestantism. In Augustine the mystic thirsting for the living God meets the sceptic who lays down reason in obedience to church authority. On one side he preaches the irresistible grace of sovereign predestination, on another a law of works which leaves no room for predestination; on one side the assurance of the church for salvation, on the other the impossibility of any assurance in this world for our election. All these ideas lie side by side in his writings and it has been a work of centuries to disentangle from them the different systems of

[1] *Monasticism and the Confessions of St. Augustine*, p. 123.
[2] Foreword to *St. Augustine* by Eleanor McDougall.

thought which have arisen in the Latin and Teutonic West from his time nearly to our own."[1]

The Council of Trent and Calvin, and many Roman Catholic and Protestant thinkers since their time, have sought to clinch an argument by a quotation from his writings. Both Catholic and Evangelical have confidently claimed him as their own. A High Churchman, making much of ecclesiastical authority, he yet had a religion that was personal to the core, a reliance on the grace of God mediated by faith alone. The Reformation has been described as the triumph of Augustine's doctrine of grace over Augustine's doctrine of the Church.

Pioneering as he was in strange seas of thought alone, it is perhaps not surprising that he had not thought everything through to a logical conclusion. It is evidence of greatness, no less than of inconsistency, that such varied schools of thought have appealed to his authority.

Augustine lived when mankind stood at one of the great cross-roads of history, and he did something to decide which way men should go. When he was born in A.D. 354 at Thagaste in what is now Algeria, the Roman Empire seemed as unshakable as the great Atlas mountains of his homeland. During his life-time the incredible happened; Rome fell before the northern invaders. As he died, the Vandals having over-run Italy were besieging his own town of Hippo.

So Augustine had his work to do while the whole order of things in which men had trusted was collapsing. It had not been wholly unworthy of trust, in spite of all its grave defects. Small blame that men's hearts failed them for fear as the foundations were being removed. Augustine died before the new order had taken shape, but among his greatest services to mankind was the fact that at such a time he could write *The City of God* (*De Civitate Dei*).

Rome itself had been sacked before he set pen to paper, and month by month as he wrote news came of the irresistible further advance of the barbarian armies. It seemed a

---

[1] *The Knowledge of God*, p. 181f.

time of unmitigated disaster. The pagans laid the blame upon the Christians. What could be expected but disaster, when the worship of the old gods was being more and more neglected? The *City of God* was addressed both to these criticisms and to men's deep-rooted sense of despair. The book is both a defence of Christianity and a Christian philosophy of history. Refuting the pagan charges and exposing the weakness and immorality of the old religion, Augustine looks to the future. A divine purpose is unfolding. Over the wreckage of Rome he sees rising another city —the City of God, without frontiers, welcoming all nations among its citizens, embracing both earth and heaven, its citizenship based upon a common faith and upon obedience to the divine law. Rome had fallen because of its sin and error. The City of God abides. Even the catastrophe of the fall of Rome is but an incident in human story and a vindication of the Divine providence. Only Christ could lead, but Christ was leading the world to its true goal.

It was a book that made history, influencing the course of ecclesiastical and political development for centuries. To give only one illustration, the *City of God* was the favourite reading of Charlemagne, and Lord Bryce declares: " It is hardly too much to say that the Holy Roman Empire is built upon the foundations of *De Civitate Dei.*"[1]

Yet it is not Augustine the theologian or the political thinker who has influenced the world most, but Augustine the Christian believer, the man redeemed by the grace of God. The *Confessions* has probably done more through the centuries to affect the lives of men than even *The City of God*. Certainly multitudes of ordinary men and women who would find his theology hard to understand, and even at times repellent, have found a lamp to their feet in his story of God's dealings with his own soul. The *Confessions* has been one of the most widely translated and widely read books in all literature,[2] and it is with the *Confessions* and

[1] *The Holy Roman Empire*, p. 94.
[2] After the first draft of this chapter had been completed a new translation by F. J. Sheed appeared. Most of the other translations are in

with the personal religious experience there recorded that this essay is concerned.

The *Confessions* is an autobiography written in the presence of God, "speaking with myself and to myself in God's presence." (IX, 4. The actual reference is to a meditation on the Fourth Psalm.) But this is more than a soliloquy. It is a conversation with God, an unbaring of the inmost self in His presence. To read it is like overhearing a man pouring out his soul in intimate prayer. It is an encounter between the human personality and the Divine, between the " I " and the " Thou." A medley of remorse and of grateful adoration, it records a long search for intellectual and moral peace and the divine guidance all along the road.

He writes with the deliberate purpose of being overheard (XI, 3). He is bearing witness to what God has done for him (XI, 1). Already he was famous and honoured throughout the world and men were eager to know about him and his life. With some it was idle curiosity. Certainly none had anticipated such an autobiography as this. "Take then, my son," he wrote in a letter, " the books which thou hast desired, the books of my Confessions. In them behold me, lest thou praise me beyond what I am; in them accept what I say of myself and not what others say of me; . . . and if anything in me wins thy approval, join me in praising not me, but Him whom I desire to be praised on my behalf. . . . And pray for me that I may not fall away." It is not without significance that he closes the autobiographical story before reaching the years of his Christian fame and influence.

His Life

Although it will involve a certain amount of repetition later, as we trace more fully the course of his spiritual

archaic English which hides the timelessness of the book from most readers. This is in modern English and taken as a whole seems to me much the best available. I have used it for my own quotations in this chapter and commend it warmly. It is published by Sheed & Ward, by whose permission I make the quotations.

experience, it will make it all more intelligible if a brief outline of his life is given at this point.

Except for five momentous years, from 383 to 388, spent in Rome and Milan, Augustine lived all his life in North Africa. His mother Monica seems to have been a very remarkable woman and exerted a powerful influence over him. There will be more to say of her later. She was a devout Christian, but his father was a pagan during Augustine's youth, and his only concern for his son was that he should have a brilliant career. While he made great sacrifices to secure for the boy the best possible schooling, he took no trouble over the development of his character. The poverty of the family necessitated Augustine's withdrawal from school at sixteen, and he remained at home for a time while his father was scraping money together for his further education. A boy of high spirits, he got mixed up with bad companions, and making all allowance for exaggeration in his later judgments of his own faults, it is evident that he led a dissipated life. " I was left," he says, " to do pretty well as I liked, and go after pleasure not only beyond the limits of reasonable discipline, but to sheer dissoluteness in many kinds of evil." (II, 3.)

Between the ages of seventeen and nineteen, through the self-denial of his parents, he went to the university of Carthage, and records in the *Confessions* (IV, 8) a happy description of his friendship with his fellow students. " All kinds of things rejoiced my soul in their company—to talk and laugh and do each other kindnesses; read pleasant books together, pass from lightest jesting to talk of the deepest things and back again; differ without rancour, as a man might differ with himself, and when most rarely dissension arose find our normal agreement all the sweeter for it; teach each other or learn from each other; be impatient for the return of the absent, and welcome them with joy on their home-coming; these and such like things, proceeding from our hearts as we gave affection and received it back, and shown by face, by voice, by the eyes, and a thousand other pleasing ways, kindled a flame which fused our very souls and of many made us one."

But he tells also a less attractive story of his relations with a wild gang who called themselves the Overturners or Wreckers—perhaps " The Rebels " would convey the idea—and gloried in escapades that went far beyond pardonable high spirits. "There was something very like the action of devils in their behaviour," says Augustine, and he tells us that though he enjoyed their companionship "for the most part," he could not bring himself to share in their worst excesses.

Augustine was a brilliant student and achieved great distinction in the school of Rhetoric, and when his course was completed was appointed to tutorial posts, first at Carthage and later at Rome. The culmination of his academic career came with his appointment to a post that might be described as " Professor and Public Orator," in Milan in 383. His removal there had quite unexpected results. A brilliant speaker himself, Augustine was attracted by the preaching of Ambrose, the Bishop of Milan. Moved at first only by the skill of his oratory, he was compelled to pay attention to the substance of the message. He discovered that he had seriously misunderstood the real nature of the Christian faith and was obliged to recognize that like many another he had exaggerated his intellectual difficulties in order to evade its moral challenge. After a fierce struggle, of which more will be said, he found at length both intellectual conviction and moral victory and was baptized by Ambrose on Easter Day, 387.

He resigned his professorship and went home to Thagaste where he spent three years in quiet study in a small community which was the germ of later monastic orders. He was persuaded to be ordained against his inclinations; partly because he was convinced of his unworthiness for the calling of the Christian ministry and partly because he was reluctant to give up his peaceful life of study. Five years later he was made Bishop of Hippo. With great devotion he gave himself to the work of preaching and pastoral care among his simple flock. He was very active in controversy with the heretics. He did much to heal the schisms of the African church and to raise the standard of the clergy by his training schools. He wrote voluminously; more than two hundred and thirty books according to his own calculation. The *Confessions* was finished about 400. From 413 to 426 he was engaged on *The City of God.* A large book on Christian doctrine, begun in 397, was not finished until 426. Hippo, in itself an unimportant and out-of-the-way diocese, became the centre of the Christian world because he was there. Requests for his advice poured in from every quarter of the compass, and he was involved in a very large correspondence. Though he became the most prominent and influential figure in the Church of his time, he declined all invitations to other posts and stayed in his diocese for thirty-five years. Even when the Vandals reached the gates of Hippo he refused to leave, and there he died, just before the city fell into their hands, in the year 430.

The Confessions

With this background we can return to the *Confessions.* Among the greatest of human writings, judged by any standard, it is not always easy reading. There is no chronological order or apparent scheme. Keen psychological analysis mingles with day dreaming. Passages of great eloquence make it easy to appreciate the fame Augustine won as an orator. Pages of rather stiff and flat argumentation are lit by the flash of an incisive phrase. Some of the prose is of the greatest beauty. One writer says that "Augustine was the great poet of the ancient Church, though just as little as Plato did he write in verse. These two go together as the great poet-philosophers of all time."[1] At the very outset comes that unforgettable saying, known to many who know nothing else of his writings: "Thou hast made us for Thyself, and our hearts are restless till they rest in Thee." That might be the text of the whole

[1] E. Norden, quoted in the *Encyclopedia of Religion and Ethics.*

book. It is the story of a restless heart that found rest in God.

God as Seeker: Man as Sinner

"Thou hast made us for Thyself": that expresses God's longing for the human soul and not only man's longing for God. To most saints and mystics the religious life is a toilsome search for God. To Augustine God was seeker rather than sought. From his own experience he knew that God takes the initiative. He would have understood to the full Francis Thompson's story of flight from the Hound of Heaven.

> I fled Him, down the nights and down the days;
> I fled Him, down the arches of the years;
> I fled Him, down the labyrinthine ways
> Of my own mind: and in the mist of tears
> I hid from Him, and under running laughter.
> Up vistaed hopes I sped:
> And shot, precipitated,
> Adown titanic glooms of chasmed fears,
> From those strong Feet, that followed, followed after.

That is Augustine in another idiom. The *Confessions* resounds with the unwearying tread of those strong Feet.

"Thou didst seek us when we sought not Thee, didst seek us indeed that we might seek Thee" (XI, 2). "You the Almighty are with me even before I am with You" (X, 4). He was like a patient refusing to accept the treatment of the physician (VI, 4). Heavy with sleep, he resented God's call to awake (VIII, 5).

In his appointment as professor at Milan and the resulting meeting with Ambrose which led to his conversion, he traces the guiding Hand. "All unknowing I was brought by God to him, that knowing I should be brought by him to God" (V, 13). Looking back, he sees that it was through the mercy of God that bitter disappointment had often attended his efforts to find satisfaction. Before he became a Christian Augustine was a very successful man. He had won fame, position, learning, love; but he was unhappy. He never knew happiness and unity of soul until he found Christ. "I was all hot for honours, money, marriage. . . . In my pursuit of these, I suffered most bitter disappointments, but in this You were good to me, since I was thus prevented from taking delight in anything not Yourself" (VI, 6, 10). "You kept stirring me with your secret good so that I should remain unquiet until You should become clear to the gaze of my soul" (VII, 8; V, 8).

As the writer of the Twenty-third Psalm traced throughout his life the shepherding of God, in the valley of the shadow as well as beside the still waters, so Augustine knew that even when he seemed to be "blown about by every wind" there was a hidden steersman at the helm (IV, 14).

In one passage he writes of the encompassing presence of God in words reminiscent of the 139th Psalm: "Let the wicked in their restlessness go from Thee and flee away. Yet Thou dost see them, cleaving through their darkness. And all the universe is beautiful about them, but they are vile. What harm have they done Thee? Or have they brought dishonour on Thy government, which from the heavens unto the latest things ot earth is just and perfect? Where indeed did they flee to when they fled from Thy face? Or where dost Thou not find them? The truth is that they fled, that they might not see Thee who sawest them. And so with eyes blinded they stumbled against Thee—for Thou dost not desert any of the things that Thou hast made—they stumbled against Thee in their injustice and justly suffered, since they had withdrawn from Thy mercy and stumbled against Thy justice and fallen headlong upon Thy wrath. Plainly they do not know that Thou art everywhere whom no place compasses in, and that Thou alone art ever present even to those that go furthest from Thee. Let them therefore turn back and seek Thee because Thou hast not deserted Thy creatures as they have deserted their Creator. Let them turn back, and behold Thou art there in their hearts, in the hearts of those that confess to Thee and cast themselves upon Thee and weep on

Thy breast as they return from ways of anguish. Gently Thou dost wipe away their tears and they weep the more and are consoled in their weeping: because Thou, Lord, and not any man that is only flesh and blood, Thou, Lord, who hast made them, dost remake them and give them comfort. But where was I when I sought after Thee? Thou wert there before me, but I had gone away from myself and I could not even find myself, much less Thee."

God beset him behind and before and kept His hand upon him. " O good Omnipotent, You who have such care for each one of us as if You had care for him alone, and such care for all as if we were all but one person " (III, 11).

If man by searching cannot find out God, Augustine was very sure that God can find man.

Man as Sinner

Against this seeking love of God was the resistance of sinful man, refusing to be found.

It is usual in most modern writings to declare that Augustine had a morbid and exaggerated sense of sin, and perhaps with some justification. Certainly he took his childish faults too seriously. One suspects the lack of a sense of proportion and of humour when he can comment on a reluctance to learn his lessons " through sheer love of play "—" so small a boy and so great a sinner " (I, 12): or exclaim " is this the innocence of boyhood? " after a recital of some not very serious and certainly quite normal boyish misdemeanours (I, 19). He almost out-Freuds the Freudians in his analysis of the jealousies of infants (I, 7).

But one cannot dispose of Augustine like that. It is impossible to escape the uneasy feeling that he was nearer the truth in his understanding of the human heart than most of us with our defective sense of sin. Certainly the New Testament is on his side. If we reject Augustine we must also reject St. Paul.

Throughout the *Confessions* Augustine reveals a deep sense of sin and unworthiness. He insists on probing into the inner motives behind his actions. A striking illustration of this self-examination occurs in a story of his boyhood. He stole some pears from a tree: not a very serious crime, say most of us, and leave it at that. But Augustine will not leave it at that, and by searching analysis of this particular act he tries to unbare the essence of sin. Why did I want to steal those pears? he asks. I was not hungry. I did not need them. There were better pears in my own home. In fact I threw the pears to the hogs when I had barely tasted them. "Our only pleasure in doing it was that it was forbidden. . . . I was evil for no object, having no cause for wrong doing, save my wrongness."

As he thinks back on the state of his mind then, he is certain that he would never have committed the theft alone. "Here then, O God, is the memory still vivid in my mind. I would not have committed that theft alone: my pleasure in it was not what I stole but that I stole: yet I would not have enjoyed doing it, I would not have done it, alone. O friendship unfriendly, unanalysable attraction for the mind, greediness to do damage for the mere sport and jest of it, desire for another's loss with no gain to oneself or vengeance to be satisfied! Someone cries 'Come on, let's do it!'—and we would be ashamed to be ashamed! Who can unravel that complex twisted knottedness? It is unclean. I hate to think of it or look at it." (II, 4, 10.)

Dr. W. M. Macgregor declared in a lecture that this passage "revealed nothing but the great man's inability to enter into the feelings of a mischievous boy." This is surely going too far, but there is at least a serious absence of any true sense of proportion.

In the Tenth Book of the *Confessions* there is a penetrating analysis of the nature of temptation. At times Augustine shows a shrinking from all pleasures of the senses, yet there is a revealing passage in which after deprecating excessive use of vestments, pictures, statues and the like in worship, he praises God for art. "I too offer my praise . . . For all that loveliness which passes through men's minds into their skilful hands comes from that supreme Loveliness which is above our souls, which my

soul sighs for day and night. From the Supreme Beauty
those who make and seek after exterior beauty derive the
measure by which they judge of it, but not the measure by
which it should be used. Yet this measure too is there,
and they do not see it: for if they did they would not
wander far from it, but would preserve their strength only
for Thee and would not dissipate it upon delights that grow
wearisome." Augustine was a reluctant ascetic. He writes
as if afraid to give rein to his sense of beauty, lest it
should carry him away into slippery places (X, 34).

He knows that pride and lust are the two great enemies
of man's soul. He has to struggle with them in himself.
Pride, the desire to show off, to win the first place, was
planted firmly in his heart even in schooldays. It made
him steal and lie and cheat. The " briars of unclean desire "
tripped him up in boyhood and clung to him through manhood. Pride and lust continued to entangle him, and pride
remained when lust was conquered. Here surely is the
Bishop speaking: " Because certain offices in human society
require the holder to be loved and feared by men, the
enemy of our true beatitude presses hard upon me, spread-
ing all about me his snares of Well done, Well done; and
while I receive praises too eagerly, I lose caution and am
caught by them, and so separate my joy from the truth and
place it in the deceitfulness of men: I delight to be praised
and feared, not for Your sake but in Your stead " (X, 36).

How can the enslaved will of sinful man turn to God?
That is no problem to the man who does not know what
sin means. But to the saints from the Apostle Paul onwards it has been the master problem of all. Like Calvin
after him, Augustine knew too much about human nature
to trifle with the question. If we cannot altogether accept
his answer, we should at least do well to recognize that it is
an attempt to answer a real question.

It was useless, declared Augustine, for man to try to be
good or to find God. The more he struggled, the tighter
drew the knots; only God could untie them. In his argument with Pelagius, the contemporary British theologian—

and still typical of British theology, say our Continental friends—Augustine's position was sharply defined. Pelagius said that men had the power to choose between good and evil. God's help is needed, but there must first be an un-aided act of the human will in order to accept the divine grace. Augustine maintained that grace was needed in order to accept grace. As a result of Adam's sin the human will was no longer free and could not free itself. Divine grace must itself bestow the liberty by which the human will can respond. Pelagius said that the initiative was taken by the human will; Augustine said it was taken by the divine will. Of His own free grace God elected some to eternal life, not for any merit in them, but for His own inscrutable reasons. All deserved death. Those whom God did not elect had therefore no ground of complaint. If grace was sovereign it was not arbitrary; God had His own reasons, even if we could not know them. Those elected were not simply chosen to be saved, they were chosen to work out their own salvation strenuously.

To Augustine this was no remote academic argument. Sin was a horrid reality in his own life and so was the powerless will. But so too was the grace of God. In what God did for himself in setting him free, producing harmony out of discord, Augustine saw what God might do for all men.

A Double Salvation

"All men know," wrote Augustine in a letter, "that I went to Italy one man and returned another." His life was divided clearly by his conversion at the age of thirty-two. In a letter afterwards he wrote: "I had destroyed myself, but He who created me, created me anew." He was born again, if ever a man was. His was a double salvation. Out of deep and long-continued intellectual and moral unrest, he was brought to right ways of thinking about God and to a right way of life.

Intellectual Salvation

All his life a deep thinker who asked big questions, it was

long before he found satisfying answers. But he found intellectual rest before he found moral victory.

A now lost book of Cicero first turned his mind to serious thoughts of God. "Quite definitely it changed the direction of my mind, altered my prayers to You, O Lord, and gave me a new purpose and ambition. Suddenly all the vanity I had hoped in I saw as worthless and with an incredible intensity of desire I longed after immortal wisdom. I had begun that journey upwards by which I was to return to You. My father was now dead two years: I was eighteen and was receiving money from my mother for the continuance of my study of eloquence. But I used that book not for the sharpening of my tongue; what won me in it was what it said, not the excellence of its phrasing." (III, 4.)

This quickened interest made him turn to the Bible, influenced by the example of his mother. But he found it flat after the majesty of Cicero. He says himself that he was too conceited to be able to appreciate the simplicity of the Scriptures (III, 5). But it seems clear that he was also repelled by the bad Latin version which was all that was then available. It was a contemporary of his own, Jerome, who produced the Vulgate, the literary Latin version.

So Augustine turned instead to Manichæism, of which he remained more or less a disciple for nine years: "stumbling in a slippery course and amid much smoke, sending out some sparks of faithfulness." Manichæism originated in Persia in the middle of the third century. It spread with remarkable rapidity, and in some quarters, not least in North Africa, it proved a strong rival to Christianity. The founder held Jesus in reverence, but, like Muhammad at a later date, was apparently not acquainted with orthodox Christianity; Manichæism was a rival religion and not a Christian heresy. It was a blend of the old Magian religion with elements drawn from Christian sources. The ancient mythology was combined with a belief in two eternally opposed kingdoms of light and darkness, good and evil. Matter was evil and a strict asceticism was inculcated. Its " church " was carefully organized on an episcopal basis, and a simple form of worship was followed. This combination of subtle speculation with simple worship and strict morality proved very attractive. Its doctrine of sin removed personal responsibility, and this also appealed to Augustine, while its subtle speculations ministered to his intellectual pride. " I held the view that it was not we that sinned, but some other nature sinning in us: and it pleased my pride to be beyond fault, and when I did any evil not to confess that I had done it, that You might heal my soul because it had sinned against You: I very much preferred to excuse myself and accuse some other thing that was in me but was not I. . . . My sin was all the more incurable because I thought I was not a sinner." (V, 10.)

Yet Augustine in after life was not ungrateful to the Manichees. In a letter addressed to them, some years before he published the *Confessions,* he wrote: " Let those treat you angrily who know not with what sighs and groans the least particle of the knowledge of God is obtained. For my part I, who after much and long continued bewilderment attained at last to the discovery of the simple truth, can on no account treat you angrily; for I must bear with you now as patiently as I had to bear with myself and I must be as patient toward you as my friends were with me when I went madly and blindly astray in your belief." Unhappily Augustine did not always show such a tolerant spirit. His later encouragement of the persecution of heretics is a grave blot upon his story.

Never wholly contented with Manichæism his disillusionment grew by degrees. At the age of thirty-one he was deeply influenced by Neoplatonism which he afterwards described as " the elder sister of Christianity." It proved to be for him the vestibule through which he entered the Christian Church. Or, to use yet another metaphor, his Christian thought was grafted on to a Neoplatonic stock, and through him it exerted a great influence on later Christian theology. In the Seventh Book of the *Confessions*

Augustine discussed at length what he learned from these writings and how they delivered him from the errors of Manichæism and prepared the way for Christianity.

As we have seen, the final step was taken under the influence of Ambrose. Attracted at first by his professional interest in the bishop's remarkable eloquence, he was led to personal acquaintance with his powerful and winning personality. He found in Ambrose one who had given up wealth and position for his faith, with a mind as good as his own and an equal rhetorical skill. Augustine was thus led for the first time to serious study of Christianity. He found that many of the beliefs which he had previously associated with Christianity and which had repelled him, were not in fact Christian beliefs at all. For example, he was astonished to find that Christianity did not attribute a human form to God. (VI, 3.)

"That man of God received me as a father. . . . I came to love him not at first as a teacher of the truth, which I had utterly despaired of finding in Your church, but for his kindness towards me. I attended carefully when he preached to the people, not with the right intention, but only to judge whether his eloquence was equal to his fame. . . . Yet little by little I was drawing closer, though I did not realize it. Thus I did not take great heed to learn what he was saying but only to hear how he said it: that empty interest was all I now had since I despaired of man's finding the way to You. Yet along with the words which I admired, there also came into my mind the subject matter, to which I attached no importance. I could not separate them. And while I was opening my heart to learn how eloquently he spoke I came to feel, though only gradually, how truly he spoke."

It was not long before Augustine's renewed study convinced him of the truth of the Christian faith.

Moral Salvation

But this intellectual conviction brought no sense of religious assurance. "I had now found the pearl of great

price, and I ought to have sold all I had and bought it.   But
I hesitated still " (VIII, 1).   " The enemy held my will. . . .
The new will which I now began to have, by which I willed
to worship You freely and enjoy You, O God, the only
certain Joy, was not yet strong enough to overcome that
earlier will rooted deep through the years.   My two wills,
one old, one new, one carnal, one spiritual, were in conflict
and in their conflict wasted my soul."   (VIII, 5.)

He now understood from his own experience the struggle
between flesh and spirit, of which St. Paul wrote.   He too
was in both camps at once.   " I no longer had the excuse
which I used to think I had for not yet forsaking the world
and serving You, the excuse namely that I had no certain
knowledge of the truth.   By now I was quite certain."

Augustine had been living for fifteen years with a woman
who was his wife in all but legal status, and had borne him
a son, Adeodatus.   His conscience troubled him about this
relationship.   He felt incapable of a celibate life.   Separation from his mistress, and marriage to some suitable bride
seemed the only course.   Why he could not marry this
much-loved mistress is never explained; probably she was
unsuitable by reason of education and social position.
When he left her, his heart was " broken and wounded and
shed blood."   The young girl to whom he became engaged
could not be married for two years.   But, writes Augustine,
" it was not really marriage I wanted.   I was simply a slave
to lust.   So I took another woman, not of course as a wife;
and thus my soul's disease was nourished."   Augustine was
made wretched and humiliated by his weakness.   He had
not been strong enough to obey the voice of his conscience.
The day was approaching when he would have to face
without flinching the truth that it was this moral issue, and
not the intellectual difficulties on which he had rather
prided himself, which was really keeping him from accept-
ing Christ as Lord.

The crisis came when a visitor related to his friend
Alypius and himself stories of the ascetic St. Anthony, and
of two young men who had recently taken the vow of

celibacy in order to serve Christ. As the visitor was speaking, writes Augustine quaintly, God took me "from behind my own back, where I had put myself all the time that I preferred not to see myself. And You set me there before my own face that I might see how vile I was. . . . I saw myself and was horrified."

Augustine was in the grip of sin and yet afraid to be free, crying for purity and yet clinging to unchastity. "Soon." "Quite soon." "Give me just a little time." So he had been answering the summons of God (VIII, 5). "Grant me chastity, but not yet. For I was afraid that You would hear my prayer too soon, and too soon would heal me from the disease of lust which I wanted satisfied rather than extinguished." (VIII, 7.)

When the visitor had gone, Augustine was in a "great tumult" of soul. He went out into the garden, "frantic in mind, in a frenzy of indignation" against himself. He had but to make a decision, to perform an act of will. Yet he found his will powerless, "twisting and turning in its chains." "What did I not say against myself, with what lashes of condemnation did I not scourge my soul to make it follow me now that I wanted to follow You. My soul hung back. It would not follow, yet found no excuse for not following. All its arguments had already been used and refuted. There remained only trembling silence: for it feared as very death the cessation of that habit of which in truth it was dying." (VIII, 7.)

Alone in the garden, "I flung myself down somehow under a certain fig tree and no longer tried to check my tears, which poured forth from my eyes in a flood, *an acceptable sacrifice to Thee.* And much I said, not in these words but to this effect: '*And Thou, O Lord, how long? How long, Lord; wilt Thou be angry for ever? Remember not our former iniquities.*' For I felt that I was still bound by them. And I continued my miserable complaining: 'How long, how long shall I go on saying to-morrow and again to-morrow? Why not now, why not have an end to my uncleanness this very hour?'

C

" Such things I said, weeping in the most bitter sorrow of my heart. And suddenly I heard a voice from some nearby house, a boy's voice or a girl's voice, I do not know : but it was a sort of singsong, repeated again and again, ' Take and read, take and read.' I ceased weeping and immediately began to search my mind most carefully as to whether children were accustomed to chant these words in any kind of game, and I could not remember that I had ever heard any such thing. Damming back the flood of my tears I arose, interpreting the incident as quite certainly a divine command to open my book of Scripture and read the passage at which I should open. For it was part of what I had been told about Anthony, that from the Gospel which he happened to be reading he had felt that he was being admonished as though what he read was spoken directly to himself : *Go, sell what thou hast and give to the poor and thou shalt have treasure in heaven; and come follow Me.* By this experience he had been in that instant converted to You. So I was moved to return to the place where Alypius was sitting, for I had put down the Apostle's book there when I arose. I snatched it up, opened it and in silence read the passage upon which my eyes first fell : *Not in rioting and drunkenness, not in chambering and impurities, not in contention and envy, but put ye on the Lord Jesus Christ and make not provision for the flesh in its concupiscences* (Romans xiii. 13). I had no wish to read further, and no need. For in that instant, with the very ending of the sentence, it was as though a light of utter confidence shone in all my heart, and all the darkness of uncertainty vanished away."

The first to be told was his mother who was " filled with triumphant exultation." To her his conversion was the greatest gift life had to offer, and indeed she felt she had nothing more to live for. The four greatest influences upon this very great man were Cicero, Plato, Ambrose— and his mother. Her belief in her son, her prayers, her love, followed him through all his moral and intellectual wanderings. " Often when Ambrose saw me," wrote

Augustine, " he would congratulate me on having such a mother." "I have no words to express the love she had for me, and with how much more anguish she was now in spiritual travail of me than when she had borne me in the flesh." (V, 9.) A few days before her fatal illness she said to him: "Son, for my own part I no longer find joy in anything in this world. What I am still to do here and why I am here I know not, now that I no longer hope for anything from this world. One thing there was, for which I desired to remain a little longer in this life, that I should see you a Catholic Christian before I died. This God has granted me in super-abundance, in that I now see you His servant to the contempt of all worldly happiness. What then am I doing here?" (IX, 10.)

After further instruction Augustine was baptized in Milan Cathedral by Ambrose, along with his friend Alypius and his son Adeodatus, then a boy of fifteen. This was on Easter Sunday, in the year 387, in Augustine's thirty-third year.

Augustine resigned his professorship and determined to return to Africa to serve his own people. He set out with his mother, but before they left Italy she fell ill and died in a few days. One of the most wonderful passages in the *Confessions*, and indeed in all literature, tells the story of that time. Here is part of his account of a conversation between them, as they looked down from a window over the garden at Ostia on the Tiber, resting, as they thought, before taking ship for Carthage. "And our conversation had brought us to this point, that any pleasure whatsoever of the bodily senses, in any brightness whatsoever of corporeal light, seemed to us not worthy of comparison with the pleasure of that eternal Light, not worthy even of mention. Rising as our love flamed upward towards that Selfsame, we passed in review the various levels of bodily things, up to the heavens themselves, whence sun and moon and stars shine upon this earth. And higher still we soared, thinking in our minds and speaking and marvelling at Your works: and so we came to our own souls, and went

beyond them to come at last to that region of richness un-
ending, where You feed Israel for ever with the food of
truth: and there life is that Wisdom by which all things are
made, both the things that have been and the things that
are yet to be. But this Wisdom itself is not made: it is as
it has ever been, and so it shall be for ever: indeed 'has
ever been' and 'shall be for ever' have no place in it, but
it simply is, for it is eternal: whereas 'to have been' and
'to be going to be' are not eternal. And while we were
thus talking of His Wisdom and panting for it, with all
the effort of our heart, we did for one instant attain to touch
it; then sighing, and leaving the first fruits of our spirit
bound to it, we returned to the sound of our own tongue, in
which a word has both beginning and ending. For what is
like to Your Word, O Lord, who abides in Himself for ever,
yet grows not old and makes all things new!

"So we said: If to any man the tumult of the flesh grew
silent, silent the images of earth and sea and air: and if the
heavens grew silent, and the very soul grew silent to herself
and by not thinking of self mounted beyond self: if all
dreams and imagined visions grew silent, and every tongue
and every sign and whatsoever is transient—for indeed if
any man could hear them, he should hear them saying with
one voice: We did not make ourselves, but He made us who
abides for ever: but if, having uttered this and so set us to
listening to Him who made them, they all grew silent, and
in their silence He alone spoke to us, not by them but by
Himself: so that we should hear His word, not by any
tongue of flesh nor the voice of an angel nor the sound of
thunder nor in the darkness of a parable, but that we
should hear Himself whom in all these things we love,
should hear Himself and not them: just as we two had but
now reached forth and in a flash of the mind attained to
touch the eternal Wisdom which abides over all: and if
this could continue, and all other visions so different be
quite taken away, and this one should so ravish and absorb
and wrap the beholder in inward joys that his life should
eternally be such as that one moment of understanding for

which we had been sighing—would not this be: *Enter thou into the joy of thy Lord?* "

This quotation fitly points to the conclusion of the whole story. Intellect, heart, will—all Augustine's personality, however subdivided—was now united in a whole-souled surrender to God. Even that is too cold a way of putting it. Augustine had fallen in love with God, with a deep, all-absorbing, passionate devotion. " The true subject (of the *Confessions*) " writes Miss McDougall, " is not the wanderings of Augustine but the love of God."[1]

Again and again he breaks off his narrative to utter exclamations of wonder and gratitude at the goodness of the Lord who had done such great things for him. They remind one of the doxologies of St. Paul, similarly breaking into the argument out of a full heart. At times indeed the *Confessions* read almost like love-letters, full of affectionate asides. Here are some of these spontaneous outcries of delight and devotion, taken almost at random. " O my supreme and good Father, Beauty of all things beautiful " (III, 6); " O God of my heart " (IV, 2); " My God and my Life and my sacred Delight (I, 4); " Light of my life " (VII, 1); " Thou light of my heart, thou bread of my inmost soul " (I, 13).

Let two paragraphs be chosen to sum it all up. " Late have I loved Thee, O Beauty so ancient and so new; late have I loved Thee! For behold Thou wert within me, and I outside; and I sought Thee outside and in my unloveliness fell upon those lovely things that Thou hast made. Thou wert with me and I was not with Thee. I was kept from Thee by those things, yet had they not been in Thee they would not have been at all. Thou didst call and cry to me and break open my deafness: and Thou didst send forth Thy beams and shine upon me and chase away my blindness: Thou didst breathe fragrance upon me, and I drew in my breath and do now pant for Thee: I tasted Thee, and now hunger and thirst for Thee: Thou didst touch me, and I have burned for Thy peace." (X, 27.) " How lovely I

[1] *St. Augustine*, p. 105.

suddenly found it to be free from the loveliness of those vanities, so that now it was a joy to renounce what I had been so afraid to lose. For You cast them out of me, O true and supreme Loveliness, You cast them out of me and took their place in me, You who are sweeter than all pleasure, yet not to flesh and blood; brighter than all light, yet deeper within than any secret; loftier than all honour, but not to those who are lofty to themselves. No, my mind was free from the cares that had gnawed it, from aspiring and getting and weltering in filth and rubbing the scab of lust. And I talked with You as friends talk, my glory and my riches and my salvation, my Lord God."

No one can be quite the same after reading this book with serious attention. Often, as one reads, one catches a glimpse of the truth about one's own little soul in the great mirror that is reflecting his. He is revealing not only himself, but the essential human heart. Like his Master, he knows what is in man.

But he writes not only of human need. He writes of the ways of the love of God with man, the same to-day as sixteen hundred years ago. A living voice speaks that compels a hearing.

III

The Letters of Samuel Rutherfurd
(1600-1661)

Wʜᴇɴ Charles II came to his throne in May, 1660, nowhere
was he welcomed more warmly than in Scotland. A fort-
night before his entry into London Charles was proclaimed
king in Edinburgh "with solempnities requisite, by ringing of bellis, roring of cannounes, touking of drumes,
dancing about the fyres, and using all uther takins of joy
for the advancement and preference of their native King."[1]
He had no subjects more zealous in their loyalty than the
men and women of Presbyterian Scotland.

But Charles himself had little love for Scotland or for
its Kirk. His stay in Scotland ten years before had been
irksome in the extreme. Criticism and advice had been
freely offered him, often in sermons he would have found
tediously long whatever their topic. He had been allowed
little personal freedom. So he carried a grudge with him
to the throne and the counsellors he gathered round him
in Scotland shared his dislike of Covenanting zeal. It was
not long before those who had been ringing the bells were
wringing their hands, to adapt Walpole's famous phrase.

On New Year's Day in 1661 a Scottish Parliament met
in Edinburgh, carefully selected to be a pliant instrument
of the king's will. Before mid-July the Drunken Parliament,
as it became known with good reason, had played havoc
with Scottish freedom and Scottish faith. With the full
tale of its crimes and follies we are not now concerned, but
only with one; it marked for execution four of the outstanding leaders of the Covenanters, among whom was
Samuel Rutherfurd, Principal of New College and Rector
of the University of St. Andrews. Not least of his offences

---

[1] Quoted in Smellie's *Men of the Covenant*, to which this whole
chapter is indebted.

was his then famous book *Lex Rex*. It was a plea for constitutional monarchy under the supreme rule of God, a denunciation of all despotism and an assertion of the sovereignty of the people. Its argument is a commonplace of modern British democracy, but it was then denounced as " full of seditious and treasonable matter." Perhaps, too, Charles had not forgotten that when he passed through St. Andrews on his way to be crowned and swear the Covenant at Scone, "Mr. Samuell Rutherfurde had a speche to him in Latin, running mutch upon what was the dewty of kings." In the autumn of 1660 all copies of *Lex Rex* that could be gathered together were publicly burned at the Mercat Cross in Edinburgh and before New College in St. Andrews. The writer of it could not have been surprised when in the spring of the following year his own turn came. He was deprived of his position and summoned to appear at the bar of the House on a charge of treason.

But his enemies had waited too long. " Tell them," said Rutherfurd to their emissaries, "that I have a summons already from a superior Judge and judicatory, and I behove to answer my first summons; and, ere your day arrives, I will be where few kings and great folks come." He was already on his death-bed. "It's no easy thing to be a Christian," he said to another, more sympathetic visitor, " but, for me, I have gotten the victory, and Christ is holding out His arms to embrace me." On March 29th, 1661, he answered the summons of his Master. His best memorial is in the volume of his collected letters published in 1664 under the title of *Joshua Redivivus or Mr. Rutherfoord's Letters,* and often reprinted since. Before me as I write lies a copy of the original edition, a little old—nearly three hundred years old—volume, with yellowing pages, much read and marked and well thumbed by generations of readers. One does not need to share all Samuel Rutherfurd's theology to be stirred by his devotion to Christ, and the urgency of his pleadings with his correspondents.

JOSHUA REDIVIVUS,

OR

MR RUTHERFOORD'S

LETTERS,

Divided in two Parts.

THE FIRST,

Containing these which were written from Aberdeen, where he was confined by a sentence of the *High Cemmiffion*, drawn forth againft him, partly upon the account of his *declining* them, partly upon the account of his *Non-Conformitie.*

THE SECOND,

Containing, fome which were written from *Anwotk*, before he was by the *Prelats* perfecution thruft from his Minif-tery ; & others upon diverfe occafions afterward from *St Andrews , London , &c.*

Now published, for the ufe of all the people of God; but more particularly, for thefe who now are, or afterward may be put to fuffering for Chrift & his caufe ; By

A wellwisher to the work, & people of God.

JOH. 16. 2. *They shall put you out of the fynagogues : Yea. the time cometh that whofoever killeth you , will think that he doeth God fervice. V. 3. And thefe things will they doe unto you, becaufe they have not known the Father , nor me.*

THESS. 1: 6. *Seeing it is a righteous thing with God , to re-compenfe tribulation to them that trouble you. V. 7. And to you who are troubled reft with us, when the Lord Iefus shall be revealed from heaven with his mighty Angels , &c.*

Printed in the Yeer cI⊃ I⊃c LXIIII

The title-page says that the letters are "now published for the use of all the people of God: but more particularly for those who now are, or may afterwards be put to suffering for Christ and His cause, by a well wisher to the work and people of God." There is no editor's name and neither printer nor publisher are mentioned. Only the date is given: "Printed in the year 1664." It was not safe to mention names in that year of grace.

By far the greater part of the letters, 215 out of 286, come from one period of his life, the two years of enforced banishment to Aberdeen from his Galloway parish. For nine years, from 1627 to 1636, he had been minister of Anwoth, where he had laboured with untiring faithfulness. "The little fair man" had been beloved by his parishioners from nobles to herd boys. "I never knew one in Scotland like him," said a brother minister of those days. "He seemed to be always praying, always preaching, always visiting the sick, always teaching in the schools, always writing treatises, always reading and studying." But the Bishop of Galloway, restored by King James, was offended by a book Rutherfurd wrote against Arminianism. He had him deposed and exiled to the far away northern city.

The hardest trial to the fervent preacher, next to his separation from his parishioners, was his "dumb Sabbaths," as he called them. He was forbidden to preach, and the Word of God was to him, as to Jeremiah, like a burning fire shut up in his bones and he was weary with forbearing and could not contain. But if his lips were closed, he was free to write, and letters poured from his pen. He wrote to the elders of his parish, eager for its welfare. He begged young men and women to give themselves to Christ's service. He gave advice to those in trouble. He sent messages of comfort to the bereaved. He wrote comradely letters of encouragement to fellow ministers, especially to those like himself under persecution or threat of it. He urged leaders of the Covenanting cause, nobles and commoners, to stand fast. And in every letter he preached Christ.

A certain merchant from London, in a later year when Rutherfurd was again free and at work in St. Andrews, returned south a changed man, "for he was before that time altogether a stranger to true religion." When his friends asked him for the news from Scotland, he told them he had "very great and good news" to tell them. He had heard three sermons. Mr. Blair at St. Andrews "showed me the majesty of God." Then he heard Rutherfurd, "and that man showed me the loveliness of Christ." Then at Irvine a third preacher, Mr. Dickson, "showed me all my heart." "The loveliness of Christ" was not the theme of that sermon only: it was the subject of all Rutherfurd's letters, and their burning and unstudied eloquence makes it clear, even if we had no other evidence, that he must have been a moving preacher.

It is true that there is much in the letters that does not appeal to modern taste, and is even at times frankly repellent. He was too fond of using the amatory metaphors of the Song of Songs and expressing his devotion to Christ in terms of physical endearment. But that was a common practice in those days, and has been deplorably frequent in mystical writings generally. It would not strike his correspondents as it strikes us. And over-emotional as he often seems to us, at least he never makes the value of religion depend upon the feelings it arouses. "Remember," he writes, "that faith is one thing and the feeling and notion of faith another; God forbid that this were good reasoning, 'No feeling, no faith.'" Nor is it in the modern fashion to remind men, often with gruesome detail, that they are mortal, and to beg them to consider how life will look from the edge of eternity. But perhaps here it is we who are too squeamish; the remembrance of our mortality might give us a better perspective for many things. Critics have also pointed at Rutherfurd's use of metaphor. Certainly it takes one's breath away at times to try to follow the changing and turning of the metaphors even within the compass of a single letter. But that is evidence of the fullness and vividness of his mind and constitutes not a little of the charm of the letters. After all, we must remember that these are spontaneous outpourings of the soul, often penned in haste for a waiting messenger, and not literary compositions for publication.

Before we look more closely at the letters it may help to fill in some facts in the outline of the author's life. Born in 1600 in Jedburgh, Samuel Rutherfurd graduated at Edinburgh in 1621. In 1623 he became a very youthful Professor of Humanity, or Latin, in the University. In 1627 he settled as minister at Anwoth. His banishment to Aberdeen, during which he was deprived of his ministerial functions, lasted from September, 1636, to February, 1638. The Glasgow Assembly of that year swept away the Bishops and restored Rutherfurd to his parish, but his ministry there closed in 1639 when he was appointed Professor of Divinity at St. Andrews. From 1643 to 1647 he was in London as one of the Scottish Commissioners to the Westminster Assembly of Divines. He took an active and important share in the work of the Assembly and was busy with his pen and in the pulpit. Presbyterianism was urged and defended against Erastian episcopalians on the one hand and Independents on the other, though he felt that the latter were " gracious men," and, " of all that differed from us came nearest to walking with God." The Scots had agreed to help the English opponents of King Charles I on condition that Presbyterianism was imposed upon England. The Independents stoutly claimed toleration for themselves, and Rutherfurd drew upon himself the defiance of no less a man than John Milton.

> Dare ye for this adjure the civil sword
> To force our consciences that Christ set free,
> And ride us with the classic hierarchy
> Taught ye by mere A.S. and Rutherfurd?

(A.S., be it noted in passing, was Professor Adam Stewart, a Presbyterian protagonist in the pamphlet warfare. " Classic hierarchy " means " government by presbyteries," *classis* being the term used in Switzerland for presbytery.) In his numerous volumes Rutherfurd had indeed been calling for the use of civil penalties against any who would not accept Presbyterianism once it had been adopted by Parliament. Few people then in any party could conceive of an ecclesiastical settlement that did not involve an imposed uniformity, though others of the Scottish commissioners disowned any intention of persecuting any dissenters who were " sound in the faith, holy in life, and not of a turbulent, or factious carriage." But though it tried the experiment, England liked presbytery as little as Scotland liked prelacy. Few now will question that Rutherfurd was wrong and John Milton right on the issue of toleration. The whole history of our land might have been different and better, if in those crucial years of the seventeenth century men had achieved some measure of mutual forbearance.

From London Rutherfurd returned to St. Andrews where he spent the rest of his life, though the universities of Utrecht and Edinburgh both tried to tempt him away. He was one of Scotland's greatest scholars and most famous preachers; an ecclesiastic and a theologian, an uncompromising controversialist, a hard debater ready to pelt and pound his adversaries, a remorseless logician. His letters were not published till after his death and probably few except his most intimate friends ever suspected that he had another, less austere and less intellectual side to his nature. They reveal a tender sympathy, a capacity for wide and varied friendship, a love of children, and more intimate still, the man's deep humility and sense of unworthiness, coupled with a profound yet simple religious faith.

It is embarrassing to turn over the pages of the *Letters,* where so many passages are worthy to be quoted. A few samples are all that is possible, chosen with a view to illustrating some of their main themes. Remember that nearly all come from the period of the Aberdeen banishment.

Rutherfurd never lets us forget that he is a Covenanter, pledged to defend " the crown rights of the Lord Jesus," for which he was an exile. He saw Scotland handed over to the rule of usurpers. Charles Stuart had his lawful rights, but he had forgotten that he held them as vassal of King Jesus. Only Christ could reign in His Church, where " tyrannizing prelates" were imposing their unscriptural sacerdotal ceremonies and intruding false ministers into the parishes in place of the deposed rightful shepherds. Over man's conscience and in God's House Christ alone was King.

"Upon my salvation I know and am persuaded it is for God's Truth and the Honour of my King and Royall Prince Jesus I now suffer."

" The eye of Christ is upon you," he writes to Lord Lowdoun. " This poor Church, your mother and Christ's spouse, is holding up her hands and heart to God for you, and doeth beseech you with tears to plead for her husband, his Kingly Scepter, and for the liberties that her Lord and King hath given to her, as to a free Kingdom, that oweth spiritual tribute to none on earth, as being the free-born Princess and daughter to the King of Kings. . . . Let Christ's Kingly office suffer no more unworthy indignities. Be valiant for your royal King Jesus, contend for him."

And to my Lord Boyd: " I am bold to write to your Lordship beseeching you by the mercies of God, by the honour of our royal and princely King Jesus, by the sorrows, tears and desolation of your afflicted mother-church, and by the peace of your conscience and your joy in the day of Christ, that your Lordship should goe on in the strength of your Lord and in the power of his might, to bestir yourself for the vindicating of the fallen honour of your Lord Jesus. O blessed hands for evermore that shall help to put the crown upon the head of Christ again in Scotland."

Many letters are in similar strain. Here is an issue on which there can be no compromise. There is no place for

" men of Gallio's naughtie faith ": no halting between two opinions for Samuel Rutherfurd.

In others it is the pastor who writes, full of concern for his shepherdless flock—if indeed, worse still, a hireling has not been put in his vacant place. " I often think that the sparrows are blessed who may resort to the house of God in Anwoth, from which I am banished." " I had but one eye and that they have put out. My one joy, next to the flower of my joyes, Christ, was to preach my sweetest, sweetest Master and the glory of His Kingdom, and it seemed no cruelty to them to put out the poor man's one eye. And now I am seeking about to see if suffering will speak my fair One's praises, and I am trying if a dumb man's tongue can raise one note or one of Zion's springs (i.e. tunes) to advance my Well-beloved's glory. Oh if He would make some glory to Himself out of a dumb prisoner! I goe with child of His word, I cannot be delivered."

There is a long letter, which needs to be read as a whole, written to be read to his congregation. Here are a few sentences to suggest its tenor. " My soul longeth exceedingly to hear how matters goe betwixt you and Christ. . . . Let me be weighed of my Lord in a just balance, if your souls lie not weighty upon me: you goe to bed and you rise with me, thoughts of your souls depart not from me in my sleep. . . . O that he who quickeneth the dead would give life to my sowing among you! " And he goes on to beseech young and old to examine themselves if they be in good earnest in Christ. He speaks of Christ's goodness to himself. He begs them to consider the pains of hell that wait for the unrepentant sinner. He has stern words for the back-slider, and words of encouragement for the faltering disciple. " Now my dear people, my joy and my crown in the Lord, let Him be your fear, seek the Lord and his face, save your souls, pray for me. . . . The prayers and blessings of a poor prisoner and your lawfull pastor be upon you."

Like Augustine, Rutherfurd looked back upon wasted years before in manhood he at last gave himself to Christ's

service. That memory lends urgency to his appeals to
young men and women. "I desire Patrick to give Christ
the flower of his life; it were good to start soon to the
way." To another young man, he writes: "There is not
such a glassy, icy and slippery piece of way betwixt you
and heaven as youth; the devil findeth in youth dry sticks
and dry coals and a hot hearthstone; and how soon can he
with his flint cast fire, and with his bellows blow it up!"

This is how he begs another to choose well the purpose
and aim of his life: "It is easy to master an arrow and to
set it right ere the string be drawn; but when once it is
shot and in the air and the flight begun, then ye have no
more power at all to command it. And therefore O what
a sweet couple are Christ and a young man!"

Here is another letter to the same purpose: "I rejoice
to hear that Christ hath run away with your young love,
and that ye are so early in the morning matched with such
a lord. Be humble and thankful for grace, and weigh it
not so much by weight as if it be true. Christ will not
cast water on your smoking coal; He never yet put out a
dim candle that was lighted at the Sun of Righteousness.
I recommend to you prayer and watching over the sins of
your youth, for I know that missive letters go between the
devil and young blood. Satan hath a friend at court in
the heart of youth, and there pride, luxury, lust, revenge,
forgetfulness of God are hired as his agents. Happy is
your soul if Christ man the house, and take the keys
Himself, and command all, as it suiteth Him full well to
rule all wherever He is. Keep Christ and entertain Him
well, cherish His grace, blow upon your own coal, and
let Him tutor you."

He writes to one correspondent who is distressed at the
slowness of his progress in the Christian life: "It is a
sweet law of the new Covenant . . . that the citizens pay
according to their means. . . . Christ taketh as poor men
may give. . . . If there be sincerity, broken summes and
little feckless obedience will be pardoned. . . . Know ye not
that our kindly Lord retaineth His good old heart yet?

He breaketh not a bruised reed nor quencheth the smoaking flax: but if the wind blow, He holdeth His hands about it till it rise to a flame."

Several letters are addressed to mourners: "The child hath but changed a bed in the garden, and is planted up higher, nearer the sun, where he shall thrive better than in this out-field moor-ground." "He is not lost to you who is found to Christ. If he hath casten his bloom and flower, the bloom is fallen in heaven in Christ's lap; and as he was lent awhile to time, so is he given now to eternity, which will take yourself; and the difference of your shipping and his to heaven and Christ's shore, the land of life, is only in some few years, which weareth every day shorter, and some short and soon reckoned summers will give you a meeting with him."

To a mother in England whose son had died in Scotland he sends a long and tender letter telling her that he himself had lost his only two children and can feel for her grief. For the boy to die in another land, where his mother could not close his eyes, is a natural sorrow to her, but no loss to him. "There is as expedite, fair, and easy a way betwixt Scotland and heaven, as if he had died in the very bed he was born in. The whole earth is his Father's; any corner of his Father's house is good enough to die in."

Here are other words of his to people in trouble. "He delighteth to take up fallen bairns and to mend broken brows: binding up of wounds is His office." "He taketh the bairns in His arms when they come to a deep water; at least, when they lose ground, and are put to swim, then His hand is under their chin." "I know we may say that Christ is kindest in His love when we are at our weakest; and that if Christ had not been to the fore in our sad days, the waters had gone over our soul." "There be many Christians, most like unto young sailors, who think the shore and the whole land doth move, when the ship and they themselves are moved; just so not a few do imagine that God moveth, and saileth, and changeth places, because their giddy souls are under sail, and subject

D

to alteration, to ebbing and flowing; but the foundation of the Lord abideth sure."

He writes from hard-won experience when he tells of the difficulties of the Christian way. "The greatest part but play with Christianity. . . . I thought it had been an easie thing to be a Christian, and that to seek God had been at the next door, but oh the windings, the turnings, the ups and the downs that He hath led me through."

"It cost Christ and all His followers sharp showers and hot sweats ere they won to the top of the mountain. But still our soft natures would have heaven coming to our bedside when we are sleeping and lying down with us, that we might goe to heaven in warm clothes; but all that came there found wet feet by the way, and sharp storms that did take the hide off their face, and found to's and fro's, and ups and downs and many enemies by the way. It is impossible a man can take his lusts (i.e. selfish desires) to heaven with him, such wares as these will not be welcome there. Oh how loath we are to forgoe our packalds and burdens that hinder us to run our race with patience! . . . O what pains and what a death is it to nature to turn me, my self, my lust, my ease, my credit, over in, my Lord, my Saviour, my King, and my God, my Lord's will, my Lord's grace."

"God hath called you to Christ's side, and the wind is now in Christ's face in this land; and seeing ye are with Him, ye cannot expect the lee side or the sunny side of the brae."

"I have heard a rumour of the prelate's purpose to banish me, but let it come if God so will; the other side of the sea is my Father's ground as well as this side."

"Christ's cross is such a burden as sails are to a ship or wings to a bird."

"I see grace groweth best in winter."

"Be patient; Christ went to heaven with many a wrong. His visage and countenance was all marred more than the sons of men. You may not be above your Master; many a black stroke received innocent Jesus, and He received no mends, but referred them all to the great court-day, when all things shall be righted."

"When we shall come home and enter to the possession of our Brother's fair kingdom, and when our heads shall find the weight of the eternal crown of glory, and when we shall look back to pains and sufferings; then shall we see life and sorrow to be less than one step or stride from a prison to glory; and that our little inch of time-suffering is not worthy of our first night's welcome home to heaven."

But the main theme and the recurrent chorus is always Christ. "There is as much in our Lord's pantry as will satisfy all His bairns, and as much wine in His cellar as will quench all their thirst. Hunger on; for there is meat in hunger for Christ: go never from Him, but fash (i.e. bother) Him (who yet is pleased with the importunity of hungry souls) with a dishful of hungry desires, till He fill you."

"How little of the sea can a child carry in his hand; as little do I take of my great sea, my boundless and running over Christ Jesus."

"Ye may yourself ebb and flow, rise and fall, wax and wane; but your Lord is this day as He was yesterday; and it is your comfort that your salvation is not rolled upon wheels of your own making, neither have ye to do with a Christ of your own shaping."

"O pity for evermore that there should be such an one as Christ Jesus, so boundless, so bottomless, and so incomparable in infinite excellency and sweetness, and so few to take Him. O ye poor dry and dead souls, why will ye not come hither with your toom (i.e. empty) vessels and your empty souls to this huge and fair and deep and sweet well of life, and fill all your toom vessels?"

Samuel Rutherfurd would be well content that that should be the last word to be quoted. On his death-bed he was heard to say again and again: "Glory in Immanuel's land." That phrase is the refrain of the well-known hymn "The sands of time are sinking," which is throughout reminiscent of many of Rutherfurd's favourite metaphors.   Mrs. Cousin tells us that she wrote it after long familiarity with his writings.

> O Christ He is the fountain,
> The deep, sweet well of love;
> The streams on earth I've tasted,
> More deep I'll drink above:
> There to an ocean fulness
> His mercy doth expand
> And glory, glory dwelleth
> In Immanuel's land.
>
> I've wrestled on toward heaven
> 'Gainst storm and wind and tide:
> Now like a weary traveller
> That leaneth on his guide,
> Amid the shades of evening,
> While sinks life's lingering sand,
> I hail the glory dawning
> From Immanuel's land.

IV

The Practice of the Presence of God

BY BROTHER LAWRENCE (1610-1691)

AFTER Pascal's death a servant discovered, sewn into his coat, a scrap of parchment which apparently he had always carried with him. It was a record in broken words of an overwhelming ecstatic experience of the Divine Presence. Among its breathless phrases is one which reads like a cry of amazement: " Not the God of philosophers and of scholars." *Non des philosophes et des savants!* The great scientist and philosopher discovered that God revealed Himself not to the wise and prudent but to babes, not to learning but to love.[1]

No more remarkable illustration of this truth can be found than in the experience of a humble and unlearned contemporary of Pascal, Nicolas Herman of Lorraine, known to us by his " name in religion " as Brother Lawrence. Born in 1610, the son of peasants, he became a soldier. At one time he narrowly escaped being put to death as a spy; later he was wounded and remained lame for the rest of his life. On leaving the army he became footman in a French household, where he admits that his clumsiness led to many breakages. At the age of forty he entered the Carmelite Order as a lay brother in the Paris monastery, and was put to work in the kitchen. Here he spent the remaining forty years of his life, the last ten being devoted to lighter duties.

The quality of his Christian life led many to seek his guidance. One of his visitors was Mons. Beaufort, Grand Vicar to Mons. de Chalons; Cardinal de Noailles. He recorded and published after his death an account of four conversations with Brother Lawrence in 1666 and 1667 and

[1] Any book on Pascal tells of the Memorial. See, for example, *The Clue to Pascal*, Cailliet, pp. 47ff.

later another little volume of his *Spiritual Maxims*. These
with sixteen letters written to unknown correspondents are
all we have, but they are enough to present a living picture
of a singularly beautiful character, who has taken his place
on the roll of great Christian mystics. Many books on the
religious life tell us only what the author has learned from
other books, and they may have their value. But these
records of Brother Lawrence are not drawn from others'
wells: they come straight from the living spring in his
own soul. They tell of the first-hand experience of the
workings of God of a man who had little access to books
and little learning. In one of the letters he says that he
did not find his manner of life in books. (*Practice*, p. 46.)
" Often he had told me," writes his reporter, " that all he
had heard others say, all that he had found in books, all
that he had himself written, seemed savourless and dull
and heavy, when compared with what faith had unfolded
to him of the unspeakable riches of God and of Jesus Christ.
. . . It is not enough to know God as a theory. . . . Our
faith must be alive." (*Maxims*, p. 31.)[1]

Brother Lawrence's conversion took place when he was
eighteen. " He told me . . . that in the winter, seeing a
tree stripped of its leaves, and considering that within a
little time the leaves would be renewed, and after that the
flowers and fruit appear, he received a high view of the
Providence and Power of God, which has never since been
effaced from his soul. That this view had perfectly set him
loose from the world, and kindled in him such a love for
God that he could not tell whether it had increased in
above forty years that he had lived since." (P, p. 3.)

This at once calls to mind the similar experience of
Jeremiah, to whom the sight of an almond tree breaking
into bud, first of the trees after the winter—" early waker "
the Hebrews called it—brought assurance of the unseen
power of God accomplishing His purposes (Jeremiah i.
11-12). Evelyn Underhill, in her great book on *Mysticism*,

---

[1] In future references P = *The Practice of the Presence of God* and M =
Spiritual Maxims.

points out that nature has often been the medium of revelation in the story of the mystics. "The mysterious vitality of trees, the silent magic of the forest, the strange and steady cycle of its life, possess in a peculiar degree the power of unleashing the human soul: are curiously friendly to its cravings, minister to its inarticulate needs." (*Op. cit.*, p. 191.) It is interesting to recall that Richard Jefferies tells in *The Story of My Heart* of his own very similar experience, also at the age of eighteen. Tennyson's "flower in the crannied wall" is another familiar illustration of the power of trees and flowers to bring to the prepared soul messages from another realm. But, of course, there must be the ready soul. Blake "who possessed in an eminent degree this form of sacramental perception" is quoted by Miss Underhill as saying: "The tree which moves some to tears of joy is in the eyes of others only a green thing that stands in the way."[1]

This vision of the Divine in nature is more often a means of illumination, of further education and enlightenment for the already awakened soul, than of conversion. But for young Nicholas Herman it was the occasion of his first conscious response to the seeking love of God.

Many of us, especially if we are not ourselves of the mystical type, are apt to be suspicious of mysticism, as a source of pious day-dreaming and unhealthy sentimentalism. That the perversion of mysticism can be very unpleasant and a very un-Christian thing is undoubted. St. John of the Cross condemns "the spiritual gluttony" which made some cherish the experience of mystic absorption, and Madame Guyon tells how sometimes she used to let her work fall from her hands and sit for hours just enjoying her peaceful feelings. Miss Underhill scathingly comments: "Here we see Madame Guyon basking like a pious tabby cat in the beams of Uncreated Light. . . . The heroic aspect of the mystic vocation is in abeyance. Those mystical impressions which her peculiar psychic make-up permitted her to receive, have been treated as a source of

[1] *Letters of William Blake*, p. 62.

personal and placid satisfactions; not as a well-spring whence new vitality might be drawn for great and self-giving activities." (*Op. cit.*, p. 247.)

But the greatest mystics show in their lives " the rhythm of adoration and work." They do not withdraw from life into idle meditation; rather they invade life armed with new creative powers. Many instances might be quoted. St. Catherine of Genoa administered a hospital. St. Teresa, too, was a brilliant administrator and a good housewife, who declared that she found God among the pots and pans. St. Vincent de Paul was a pioneer of organized charity. Elizabeth Fry, humanizing the " wild beasts " in Newgate Jail, and Mary Slessor ruling and converting savage peoples in Calabar, were true mystics. The life they received flowed through them to others.[1]

Certainly it was always so with Brother Lawrence. For him the Presence of God brought added efficiency and faithfulness in the performance of the most uncongenial mundane tasks. Lately, he told his reporter, he had been sent to Burgundy to buy wine for the monastery, " which was a very unwelcome task for him, because he had no turn for business and because he was lame, and could not go about the boat but by rolling himself over the casks. That, however, he gave himself no uneasiness about it, nor about the purchase of the wine. That he said to God, *It was His business he was about,* and that he afterwards found it very well performed." (P, p. 13.)

" So, likewise, in his business in the kitchen (to which he had naturally a great aversion), having accustomed himself to do everything there for the love of God and with prayer upon all occasions for His grace to do his work well, he had found everything easy, during fifteen years he had been employed there." (P, p. 14.) "That the most excellent method he had found of going to God, was that of doing our common business without any view of pleasing men, and (as far as we are capable) purely for the love of God. That it was a great delusion to think that the times of

[1] See Evelyn Underhill, *The Life of the Spirit,* and especially Chap. II.

prayer ought to differ from other times: that we are as strictly obliged to adhere to God by action in the time of action, as by prayer in its season." (P, p. 28.) " That he was more united to God in his outward employments, than when he left them for devotion in retirement." (P, p. 22.)

Brother Lawrence did nothing more sensational than to walk with God about a monastery kitchen for nearly forty years. Yet the story of his example there and a few pages of his conversations with a friend have helped others through three hundred years. Let us listen to him as he speaks most intimately of his secret.

Brother Lawrence did not easily arrive at peace in the knowledge of God's love. Like John Bunyan he was for long tormented by fears that he was eternally damned. For ten years he tells us that he " suffered much." " It seemed to me that the creatures, reason and God Himself, were against me." (P, p. 49.) But he found himself at last " changed all at once; and my soul which, till that time, was in trouble, felt a profound inward peace, as if she were in her centre and place of rest. Ever since that time I walk before God simply, in faith, with humility and with love; and I apply myself diligently to do nothing and think nothing which may displease Him. . . . I would not take up a straw from the ground against His order, or from any other motive but purely that of love to Him.

" I have quitted all forms of devotion and set prayers but those to which my state obliges me. And I make it my business only to persevere in His holy presence, wherein I keep myself by a simple attention, and a general fond regard to God, which I may call an actual presence of God; or, to speak better, an habitual, silent and secret conversation of the soul with God, which often causes in me joys and raptures inwardly and sometimes also outwardly, so great, that I am forced to use means to moderate them, and prevent their appearance to others. In short, I am assured beyond all doubt that my soul has been with God these thirty years." (P, p. 50ff.)

At times Brother Lawrence expresses an assurance of not

only believing but seeing, of an habitual consciousness of the presence of God. "I see Him in such a manner as might make me say sometimes, I believe no more, but I see." (P, p. 95. See also M, pp. 25, 26.)

What intimacy of experience must lie behind a passage like this from one of his letters. "I consider myself as the most wretched of men, full of sores and corruption, who has committed all sorts of crimes against his King; touched with a sensible regret I confess to Him all my wickedness, I ask His forgiveness, I abandon myself in His hands, that He may do what He pleases with me. This King full of mercy and goodness, very far from chastising me, embraces me with love, makes me eat at His table, serves me with His own hands, gives me the key of His treasures; He converses and delights Himself with me incessantly, in a thousand and a thousand ways, and treats me in all respects as His favourite. It is thus I consider myself from time to time in His holy presence."

To such heights as these few attain. But there are in these little books a deep spiritual wisdom and words of practical advice of great service to those of us who live on the lower levels. Perhaps the teaching of Brother Lawrence may be set out under four headings.

(*a*) In harmony with the characteristic teaching of the mystics generally, he urges that the beginning of the Christian life consists of *an act of renunciation,* surrender and dedication to the will of God. "All consists in one hearty renunciation of everything which we are sensible does not lead to God." (P, p. 25.) He writes this in a letter to a correspondent who has begged him to tell how he arrived at his habitual sense of God's presence; writing, he says, with great reluctance and counting upon her promise not to let the letter be seen by anyone else. "Having found in many books different methods of going to God, and divers practices of the spiritual life, I thought this would serve rather to puzzle me, than facilitate what I sought after, which was nothing but how to become wholly God's. This made me resolve to give the all for the all: so after having given myself wholly to God, to make all the satisfaction I could for my sins, I renounced for the love of Him everything that was not Him : and I began to live as if there was none but He and I in the world." (P, p. 42). So in one of the conversations he said " that there needed neither art nor science for going to God, but only a heart resolutely determined to apply itself to nothing but Him, or for His sake, and to love Him only." (P, p. 24.) " That we ought, once for all, heartily to put our whole trust in God, and make a total surrender of ourselves to Him, secure that He would not deceive us." (P, p. 29.)

(*b*) Having thus surrendered to the will of God, we must continue to "*practise His presence.*" He returns to this again and again. " The presence of God : a subject which in my opinion contains the whole spiritual life." (P, p. 69.) " Were I a preacher, I should above all other things preach the practice of the presence of God; and were I a director I should advise all the world to it : so necessary do I think it, and so easy too." (P, p. 70.)

" We cannot escape the dangers which abound in life without the actual and continual help of God; let us then pray to Him for it continually. How can we pray to Him without being with Him? How can we be with Him but in thinking of Him often? And how can we often think of Him, but by a holy habit which we should form of it? You will tell me that I am always saying the same thing : it is true." (P, p. 86.)

• The *Spiritual Maxims* contains a fuller and more connected summary of what this practice of God's presence meant to Brother Lawrence, and it will be helpful to quote it here.

" That practice which is alike the most holy, the most general, and the most needful in the spiritual life is the practice of the Presence of God. It is the schooling of the soul to find its joy in His divine companionship, holding with Him at all times and at every moment humble and loving converse, without set rule or stated method, in all time of our temptation and tribulation, in all time of our

dryness of soul and disrelish of God, yes, even when we fall
into unfaithfulness and actual sin. . . . By thus keeping
heart and mind fixed on God, we shall bruise the head of
the evil one, and beat down his weapons to the ground."

" Since you cannot but know that God is with you in all
that you undertake, that He is at the very depth and centre
of your soul, why should you not thus pause an instant
from time to time in your outward business, and even in
the act of prayer, to worship Him within your soul, to praise
Him, to entreat His aid, to offer Him the service of your
heart and give Him thanks for all His loving kindnesses
and tender mercies."

" To worship God in spirit and in truth means to offer to
Him the worship that we owe. God is a Spirit; therefore
we must worship Him in spirit and in truth,—that is to say,
by presenting to Him a true and humble spiritual worship
in the very depth of our being. God alone can see this
worship, which, offered unceasingly, will in the end become
as it were natural, and as if He were one with our soul, and
our soul one with Him: practice will make this clear.

" To worship God in truth is to acknowledge Him to be
what He is, and ourselves as what in fact we are. To
worship Him in truth is to acknowledge with heart-felt
sincerity what God in truth is,—that is to say, infinitely
perfect, worthy of infinite adoration, infinitely removed
from sin, and so of all the divine attributes. That man is
little guided by reason.who does not employ all his powers
to render to this great God the worship that is His due.

" Furthermore, to worship God in truth is to confess that
we live our lives entirely contrary to His will, and contrary
to our knowledge, that, were we but willing, He would fain
make us conformable to Him. Who will be guilty of such
folly as to withhold even for a moment the reverence and
the love, the service and the unceasing worship that we
owe to Him."

(*c*) He calls for resoluteness and perseverance in the
Christian life: we must *practise* the presence of God if we
would have it. He urges us to speak to God, frankly and

plainly, with great simplicity and whenever we feel moved to praise Him or need His aid. " That we might accustom ourselves to a continual conversation with Him, with freedom and in simplicity. That we need only to recognize God intimately present with us to address ourselves to Him every moment." (P, p. 25.) "Lift up your heart to Him, sometimes even at your meals, and when you are in company: the least little remembrance will always be acceptable to Him. You need not cry very loud; He is nearer to us than we are aware of. It is not necessary for being with God to be always at church; we may make an oratory of our heart, wherein to retire from time to time, to converse with Him in meekness, humility, and love. Everyone is capable of some familiar conversation with God, some more, some less. He knows what we can do. Let us begin then."

And here is a message he sent to a soldier on active service. He urged him " to put all his trust in Him who accompanies him everywhere; let him think of Him the oftenest he can, especially in the greatest dangers. A little lifting up of the heart suffices; a little remembrance of God, one act of inward worship, though upon a march and sword in hand, are prayers which, however short, are nevertheless very acceptable to God; and far from lessening a soldier's courage in occasions of danger they best serve to fortify it. Let him then think of God the most he can; let him accustom himself, by degrees, to this small but holy exercise; nobody perceives it, and nothing is easier than to repeat often in the day these little internal adorations." It is perhaps not superfluous to remember that Brother Lawrence had himself seen active service. But this is good advice not for soldiers alone.

To hold oneself thus constantly in the remembrance of the presence of God is not easy. We should not wonder if at first we often failed. But " by often repeating these acts they become habitual, and the presence of God is rendered as it were natural to us " (P, p. 45). When he had failed, he had asked pardon, and without being discouraged had set his mind right again, and continued his exercise of the presence of God. " Thus by rising after my falls and by frequently renewed acts of faith and love, I am come to a state, wherein it would be as difficult for me not to think of God, as it was at first to accustom myself to it." (P, p. 35.) " We must always work at it, because not to advance in the spiritual life is to go back." (P, p. 66.) Of one enthusiastic disciple who expected the way of Christian growth to be quick and smooth, he remarked, " She seems to me full of goodwill, but she would go faster than grace. One does not become holy all at once." (P, p. 84.)

Particularly does Brother Lawrence urge perseverance and discipline in face of the obstacles of disinclination and dryness and wandering thoughts that beset all Christians at times. " You tell me nothing new," he writes to one correspondent. " You are not the only one that is troubled with wandering thoughts " (P, p. 80). It is helpful and even healthily humbling, to realize that our difficulties are not peculiar or remarkable but " common to man " (1 Corinthians x. 13). He said " that there needed fidelity in those drynesses or insensibilities and irksomeness in prayer, by which God tries our love to Him; that *then* was the time for us to make good and effectual acts of resignation " (P, p. 6). The masters of the spiritual life all unite in telling us that such distractions are inevitable and must be met with a tranquil mind and a renewed turning of the heart to God. They may spring from an imperfectly dedicated soul, but they may no less be natural and innocent, due perhaps to weariness or illness, calling for rest rather than self-reproach. They may even be the voice of God pointing us to some task that needs to be undertaken, but which perhaps we have shirked. Brother Lawrence wisely tells us that very likely they arise from an undisciplined mind, which is allowed to wander from its proper task at other times, as well as at the time of prayer. " One way to recollect the mind easily in the time of prayer and preserve it more in tranquillity, is not to let it wander too far at other times." (P, p. 82.)

"If your mind sometimes wander and withdraw itself from God, do not much disquiet yourself for that; trouble and disquiet serve rather to distract the mind, than to re-collect it; the will must bring it back in tranquillity; if you persevere in this manner, God will have pity on you." (P, p. 81.)

(*d*) It seems that Brother Lawrence found little help in elaborate systems and schemes of meditation and prayer. He engaged in the set times of worship provided by the routine of the monastery, but the heart of the religious life lay less there, for him, than in this constant endeavour to set himself in the presence of God, at all times and in all circumstances. We quoted above his statement that he found the different methods and divers practices set out in books rather a puzzle than a help. In another letter he says, "I have quitted all forms of devotion and set prayers but those to which my state obliges me. And I make it my business only to persevere in His holy presence, wherein I keep myself by a simple attention." In one of the conversations he said that he could never regulate his devotion by certain methods as some do. (P, p. 16.) "Many do not advance in the Christian progress, because they stick in penances and particular exercises, while they neglect the love of God, which is the end." (P, p. 24.)

Some of us who find schemes of prayer a burden rather than a help may find encouragement here; though we shall do well to remember that we are not Brother Lawrences, and to make sure that it is not slackness and lack of discipline that causes us to shrink from systems. All of us may at times need the reminder that all methods are means and not ends.

(*e*) Perhaps most helpful of all to most of us is the fact that it was in a kitchen that Brother Lawrence learned to practise the presence of God. He consecrated his pots and pans to the divine service. He can show us how to live for God in our kitchen, or office, or factory. Exhortation from a safe distance that we should "make drudgery divine" is apt to be irritating. But Brother Lawrence was no theorist.

He did the daily work of a kitchen for forty years and did it so that men sought his guidance on Christian living.

"We ought not to be weary of doing little things for the love of God, who regards not the greatness of the work, but the love with which it is performed." (P, p. 29.) "The most excellent method he had found of going to God, was that of doing our common business without any view of pleasing men (see Ephesians vi. 6), and (as far as we are capable) purely for the love of God." (P, p. 28.)

Here is the concluding passage from the *Conversations*. It speaks for itself. "As Brother Lawrence had found such an advantage in walking in the presence of God, it was natural for him to recommend it earnestly to others; but his example was a stronger inducement than any arguments he could propose. His very countenance was edifying; such a sweet and calm devotion appearing in it, as could not but affect the beholders. And it was observed that in the greatest hurry of business in the kitchen, he still preserved his recollection and his heavenly-mindedness. He was never hasty nor loitering, but did each thing in its season, with an even uninterrupted composure and tranquillity of spirit. 'The time of business,' said he, 'does not with me differ from the time of prayer; and in the noise and clatter of my kitchen, while several persons are at the same time calling for different things, I possess God in as great tranquillity as if I were upon my knees at the Blessed Sacrament.'" (P, p. 36f.)

V

The Pilgrim's Progress

BY JOHN BUNYAN (1628-1688)

Not the least of the reasons why the *Pilgrim's Progress* has been more widely read than any book but the Bible is just the sheer interest of it. Here is a tale that, in Sidney's familiar words, "holdeth children from play and old men from the chimney corner." It is not really a book for children and was never meant to be: yet they make it theirs. I knew one quite ordinary boy who read it through five or six times and would not be put off with any abridged version for children, which his parents thought might be more palatable, and indeed better for him. He must have skipped some of the sermonizing, as perhaps most readers do. But he found it a grand story and whatever more *Pilgrim's Progress* may be, it is certainly that. Dr. Johnson remarked to Boswell that *Don Quixote*, *Robinson Crusoe*, and the *Pilgrim's Progress* were the only three books that a reader might wish longer.

It is probably a sound rule that what an author does not enjoy writing his readers will not enjoy reading. Bunyan certainly wrote this with pleasure and a certain abandon. Indeed, like many works of genius it almost seemed to be writing itself. In his Apology for the book, Bunyan tells us that he was engaged in composing another work.

> And thus it was: I writing of the way
> And race of.saints, in this our gospel day
> Fell suddenly into an allegory
> About their journey and the way to glory.

Ideas came crowding in upon him " like sparks that from the coals of fire do fly." He had to put these attractive fancies resolutely on one side till he had completed his more serious, and as he thought, more important task. Then to gratify and divert himself—his own words—he returned in vacant seasons to his scribble.

> Thus I set pen to paper with delight,
> And quickly had my thoughts in black and white.
> For having now my method by the end,
> Still as I pulled, it came; and so I penned
> It down: until it came at last to be,
> For length and breadth, the bigness which you see.

Bunyan was already a writer of some note in his own circles and the *Pilgrim's Progress* was in fact his twenty-fourth book. But when he showed this to his friends it made some of them shake their heads. Others urged him to publish and he sided with them, contenting himself with his spirited Apology as a preface. He had at any rate, he pointed out, the best of precedents for presenting religion in story form. That some remained critical can be gathered from the enterprise of a gentleman, signing himself T.S., who undertook to correct its faults. He found the original altogether too light-hearted in its treatment and not sufficiently doctrinal. He had written his revision "in such serious and spiritual phrases that may prevent that lightness and laughter which the reading of some passages (in Bunyan's book) occasions in some vain and frothy minds." Those who have seen one of the three surviving copies assure us that T.S. succeeded in his object.[1]

Why is it that the *Pilgrim's Progress* has established itself as a classic of English literature and won the affection of many to whom Bunyan's theology is unattractive or even repugnant? For he is a dull soul who is not captured from the very first words: "As I walked through the wilderness of this world I lighted on a certain place where was a Den"—my jail, explains Bunyan in the margin— "and I laid me down in that place to sleep, and as I slept I dreamed a Dream." With unflagging interest we follow the man in rags with his burden until the gates of the

[1] See John Brown, *John Bunyan*, p. 258.

Celestial City open to let him in. "I looked in after them and behold, the City shone like the sun; the streets also were paved with gold; and in them walked many men, with crowns on their heads, palms in their hands, and golden harps to sing praises withal. . . . And after that they shut up the gates: which when I had seen, I wished myself among them." There is magic in the story and magic in the telling. Where does it come from?

In large part perhaps from its reality. Sir Sidney Lee has written of its " stirring and sustained human interest " and calls it " the greatest example of allegory in literature." But Bunyan's characters are not just allegorical figures with appropriate names. They are flesh and blood, not abstract virtues and vices. The names are admirable, and often amusing. For example, there is Mr. Talkative, the son of Saywell of Prating Row, or the brisk lad Ignorance of the county of Conceit, or the young woman whose name was Dull. Look too at the names of the " honourable friends " of the " noble prince Beelzebub," of whom Faithful had spoken contemptuously: "the Lord Old Man, the Lord Carnal Delight, the Lord Luxurious, the Lord Desire of Vain Glory, my old Lord Lechery, Sir Having Greedy, with all the rest of our nobility." The characters seldom stay long with us, but they become vivid personalities before they go, though often drawn in a few strokes with the economy of line of the great artist. As an extreme case of rapidity of portraiture take the jury at Vanity Fair, and their private consultation before the verdict: only a sentence for each but it is enough. " Then went the jury out, whose names were Mr. Blindman, Mr. No-good, Mr. Malice, Mr. Love-lust, Mr. Live-loose, Mr. Heady, Mr. High-mind, Mr. Enmity, Mr. Liar, Mr. Cruelty, Mr. Hate-light and Mr. Implacable; who every one gave in his private verdict against (Faithful) among themselves, and afterwards unanimously concluded to bring him in guilty before the judge. And first among themselves, Mr. Blindman, the foreman, said, I see clearly that this man is a heretic. Then said Mr. No-good, Away with such a fellow from the earth. Ay, said Mr. Malice, for I hate the very looks of him. Then said Mr. Love-lust, I could never endure him. Nor I, said Mr Live-loose, for he would always be condemning my way. Hang him, hang him, said Mr. Heady. A sorry scrub, said Mr. High-mind. My heart riseth against him, said Mr. Enmity. He is a rogue, said Mr. Liar. Hanging is too good for him, said Mr. Cruelty. Let's despatch him out of the way, said Mr. Hate-light. Then said Mr. Implacable, Might I have all the world given me, I could not be reconciled to him; therefore let us forthwith bring him guilty of death. And so they did."

Unforgettable is the witty picture of Mr. By-ends. Among his kindred were my Lord Turn-about, my Lord Time-server, and Mr. Facing-both-ways. The parson of the parish, Mr. Two-tongues, was his mother's own brother. Yet his " great grand-father was but a water-man, looking one way and rowing another." Mr. By-ends explained to Christian that " we somewhat differ in religion from those of the stricter sort, yet but in two small points : First, we never strive against wind and tide. Secondly, we are always most zealous when Religion goes in his silver slippers; we love much to walk with him in the street, if the sun shines and the people applaud him."

Some of the most living characters are to be found in the often depreciated Second Part; a gentler and more mellow tale, showing a kindlier judgment of mankind than the sterner First Part. Here are Great Heart and Valiant-for-Truth with his right Jerusalem blade, whom Cromwell would have been glad to see among his Ironsides, and noble Puritan women in Christiana and Mercy. And as foils to their strength are a group with whom Bunyan deals gently : Mr. Fearing, who had a Slough of Despond in his mind, Mr. Ready-to-talk, Mr. Despondency, and his daughter Miss Much-afraid.

Those who cherish the caricature of Puritanism as a glum business that frowned on pleasure and had never learned how to smile, should take note of some recurring notes in this Puritan book. With all its seriousness, and

THE
Pilgrim's Progreſs
FROM
THIS WORLD,
TO
That which is to come:

Delivered under the Similitude of a

DREAM

Wherein is Diſcovered,
The manner of his ſetting out,
His Dangerous Journey; And ſafe
Arrival at the Deſired Countrey.

I have uſed Similitudes, Hoſ. 12. 10.

By *John Bunyan.*

Licenſed and Entred according to Order.

LONDON,
Printed for *Nath. Ponder* at the *Peacock*
in the *Poultrey* near *Cornhil*, 1678.

Title-Page of the First Edition of
'THE PILGRIM'S PROGRESS.'
1678.

not forgetting its sternness and sadness, it is pervaded by a quiet sense of humour; indeed, as we have seen, some of his contemporaries complained of it.   There is music in it, and songs, and good eating, and riddles, and perhaps most surprising of all, a dance.   The pilgrims are making merry over the downfall of Giant Despair.   "Now Christiana, if need was, could play upon the viol, and her daughter Mercy upon the lute; so since they were so merry disposed, she played them a lesson, and Ready-to-halt would dance.   So he took Despondency's daughter, Much-afraid, by the hand and to dancing they went in the road.   True, he could not dance without one crutch in his hand, but I promise you, he footed it well: also the girl was to be commended, for she answered the music handsomely."

Robert Louis Stevenson, no mean judge, has praised Bunyan's character drawing, and the wide range of his imagination: "Trivial talk over a meal, the dying words of heroes, the delights of Beulah or the Celestial City, Apollyon or my Lord Hate-good, Great Heart and Mr. Worldly Wiseman, all have been imagined with the same clearness, all written of with equal gusto and precision." In more recent days Mr. George Bernard Shaw, in the Epistle Dedicatory to *Man and Superman,* compares Shakespeare's ability to paint character with that of Bunyan, to the former's discredit.   And making all allowance for Mr. Shaw's delight in having a crack at Shakespeare he is clearly expressing a deliberate literary judgment. Elsewhere he writes: "All that you miss in Shakespeare you find in Bunyan to whom the true heroic came quite obviously and naturally."[1]

"Allegory" does not convey the right suggestion.   To say, as has often been said, that Bunyan was one of the founders of the English novel is to convey a truer picture of the impression that *Pilgrim's Progress* makes.   Here and in *The Life and Death of Mr. Badman,* Bunyan has written the first great English novels.   Mr. Badman's story is a faithful and minute account of the life of a middle-

[1] G. B. Shaw, *Dramatic Opinions,* Vol. 2, p. 142.

class scoundrel in the reign of Charles II. In its convincing local colour and abundance of circumstantial detail it rivals Defoe. *Pilgrim's Progress* is of course the prince of allegories, but its characters are men and women of flesh and blood, not ticketed lay figures; just as the scenery and surroundings of the story are those of his native county visited in the pursuit of his trade.[1] The characters have passed into the number of world's acquaintances and are more real than many of the personages of history.

Bunyan describes men and women as he had seen and known them. He went about with his ears and eyes open. In his admirable standard biography, Dr. Brown has reprinted many extracts from the Church Book of the congregation in Bedford of which Bunyan became pastor. In its privacy there are sometimes recorded frank pictures of the faithfulness and failures of Bunyan's parishioners. In *Pilgrim's Progress* are seventeenth-century folk of like habit and temper. He depicted the people of his own day as he saw them and he could have given a personal name to most of them. There is Great Heart, warrior and man of prayer, typical of not a few of the Puritan soldiers of Naseby and Worcester.[2] There is the "parson of the parish, Mr. Two Tongues," and Lord Time Server; Bunyan had not far to go to find them. The trial of Faithful is a picture from the life of the times as Bunyan knew it to his cost. Bunyan's men and women are painted as they really are, with the trappings removed, and we recognize them to-day.

Pilgrim's Progress is a grand story about real people— for all their allegorical names. But that is only part of its attractiveness.

Another part is undoubtedly Bunyan's command of English. He was no poet and few of the verses he inserts

[1] To say, truthfully enough, that Bunyan was a tinker is to suggest to modern readers that he was a disreputable tramp. Bunyan, like his people for generations before him, was an established village craftsman, plying an indispensable trade.

[2] It is now established that Bunyan spent two and a half years as a soldier in the Parliamentarian army in the Civil War. See *John Bunyan* by Brown. Tercentenary edition, p. 46ff.

with too lavish a hand are a success. For the most part they are sadly prosaic. Yet the preface has some good lines, and there are one or two memorable verses, notably " Who Would True Valour See," lately come to its own in our hymn-books; and three of Bunyan's poems are in De La Mare's anthology, *Come Hither.* But of prose Bunyan was certainly a master. George Saintsbury[1] says that he had " one of the greatest gifts of phrase—of picking up the right word or right half-dozen words—that man has ever had." His style is Biblical, but not in the sense of deliberate imitation, and though he can quote with effect, he seldom sets out a selection of texts strung together. As John Richard Green says, "he had lived in the Bible till its words became his own." The Authorized Version, " the most majestic thing in our literature, and the most spiritually living thing we inherit, was for five centuries and more the one great piece of literature which gave something of a common form, and common dignity, to the thought and speech of the people."[2] In the thought and speech of Bunyan it flowered into a masterpiece of English and supremely in his *Grace Abounding* and his *Pilgrim's Progress.* He can be simple, direct, forceful, colloquial; but he can equally, when the theme requires it, write with a moving and beautiful eloquence. And as Augustine went to hear Ambrose for the beauty of his speaking but stayed to accept his Christian faith, so Bunyan read as literature has often won a hearing for his message.

In a book written during the closing months of his life, Bunyan declares that he has not " fished in other men's waters; my Bible and Concordance are my only library in my writings."[3] Elsewhere he says, " I was never out of the Bible." It was his homeland, and as familiar as the lanes of Bedfordshire.

One cannot help thinking that he might have got even more out of the Bible if he had not been at the mercy of

[1] *Short History of English Literature.*
[2] *The Teaching of English in England.* 1921.
[3] Quoted John Brown, p. 364.

a literalism which made collections of texts out of books, which treated all parts as of equal spiritual worth, and found text warring against text in a fashion that drove him to despair. The words hid the Word, and in Bunyan's tempestuous days of search after God, His loving heart was too often obscured by an unBiblical theory of inspiration. Bunyan's view of the Bible, taken together with his high-strung temperament, made intense spiritual conflict inevitable. Yet he had one inestimable qualification for Bible study which kept him from wandering far astray. "The true interpreter of the Bible," it has been said, "is neither the Higher Criticism nor an authoritative Church, but the evangelical experience of an awakened heart."[1]

For the power of *Pilgrim's Progress* lies also in the sincerity and earnestness of the writer, who is not just making up a story or composing literature, but preaching a Gospel. He enjoyed telling the tale and confesses it. But he warns the reader, in the Conclusion to the First Part, not to play with the outside of his dream but to examine the substance. He wrote for more than amusement—his own or the reader's. "Bunyan's glory is that he was at one and the same time a Puritan of living conviction and an artist of irrepressible genius, and that in him the two elements for once coalesced. . . . To Bunyan art is not everything, art indeed is nothing. He is an artist only because he cannot help being one."[2]

Sir Sidney Lee called the *Pilgrim's Progress* the epic of Puritanism, and Puritanism, whatever else may be said of it, was the creed of men in deadly earnest—about democracy, and human rights and the worth of the soul and the judgment of God. Most people to-day find something strange in both Bunyan's intense religious concern and in his theology. Neither were strange to his contemporaries. His theology, in its essence, was that of the best minds of Protestant England and Europe. Indeed one may go a good deal further than that. It will not do to blame

---

[1] R. H. Coats, *Types of English Piety*, p. 88.
[2] J. W. Mackail, *John Bunyan*, pp. 17-19.

Calvinistic Puritanism for Bunyan's spiritual torments. Saul of Tarsus, Brother Lawrence, Newman and Samuel Johnson are four personalities sufficiently different from one another and from Bunyan; yet each went through experiences not unlike his. Many parallels could be drawn, Catholic as well as Protestant, Arminian as well as Calvinist.

Bunyan's attitude to the Bible was shared by all his generation. It was a belief, says Froude,[1] "not admitted only by the intellect but accepted and realized by the imagination. No one questioned it, save a few speculative thinkers in their closets. The statesman in the House of Commons, the judge on the Bench, the peasant in a midland village, interpreted literally by this rule the phenomena which they experienced or saw. They not only believed that God had miraculously governed the Israelites but they believed that as directly and immediately He governed England in the seventeenth century."

"The lonely figure of the first paragraph in *Pilgrim's Progress*—the poor man seeking salvation with tears, with no guide save the Bible in his hand . . . is the representative Puritan of the English Puritan epoch. . . . That man multiplied, congregated, regimented, was a force of tremendous potency, to make and to destroy. It was the force by which Oliver Cromwell and George Fox and John Wesley wrought their wonders, being men of a like experience themselves."[2]

But if *Pilgrim's Progress* is the epic of Puritanism, it is also the epic of John Bunyan, the Odyssey of his own soul's travels. He read his own heart as well as the Bible.[3] Few men even among the Puritans had so tense and soul rending an experience to record as Bunyan told in *Grace Abounding to the Chief of Sinners. Pilgrim's Progress* is *Grace Abounding* retold in story form. The correspon-

---

[1] *Bunyan*, p. 4.
[2] Trevelyan, *English Social History*, p. 234.
[3] " Foole, said my Muse to mee, look in thine heart and write.' Sidney's *Ars Poetica*.

dences are many. Note only this rough sketch of the Slough of Despond in *Grace Abounding*: "I would in these days, often in my greatest agonies, even flounce towards the promise, as the horses do towards sound ground that yet stick in the mire." Venables[1] speaks of "the sudden alternations of hopes and fears, the fierce temptations, the torturing illusions, the strange perversions of isolated scraps of Bible language—texts torn from their context—the harassing doubts as to the truth of Christianity, the depths of despair and the elevations of joy," which characterized Bunyan's own spiritual pilgrimage. They are all depicted in the allegory.

Winning salvation was a stern business. Interpreter showed Christian how "a man of a very stout counten-ance" had to hack his way "most fiercely" through his armed opponents, giving and receiving many wounds before he could gain the palace and win eternal glory. And Christian spoke for Bunyan when he "smiled and said, I think verily I know the meaning of this."

It was natural to Bunyan to dramatize his own experi-ences and spiritual conflicts. He had what might now be called a visual and aural imagination. He heard voices, saw visions, dreamed dreams. He materialized his tempta-tions. He might well have joined Luther in throwing an inkpot at the devil. When he thought and read about the scenes of our Lord's life on earth, it was more than an easy metaphor for him to say that he "saw" them. "Me-thought I saw as if I had seen Him born, as if I had seen Him grow up, as if I had seen .Him walk through this world from the cradle to His cross, to which also when He came I saw how gently He gave Himself to be hanged and nailed on it for my sins and wicked doings."

There has been much debate about these "sins and wicked doings." The reader of *Grace Abounding* might be pardoned for picturing Bunyan as an evil and loose living character. Yet Bunyan himself vehemently denies that he was ever drunk or unchaste. To play tip-cat on the

[1] *Life of John Bunyan*, p. 43.

village green on Sunday, at a time when very few thought such Sunday games in any way wrong, or to share in ringing the chimes in the village church, can hardly be regarded as serious sins, though they exercised his tyrannical conscience greatly. Bunyan's greatest faults seem to have been sins of speech, of swearing and blaspheming. He tells of how he was once reproved by a foul-mouthed woman for passing all bounds in coarse language. His gifts of imagination and command of words were put to bad use in his youth. And if bell-ringing and games, innocent in themselves, had for whatever reason come to offend his moral sense, then *for him* it was sin to do what his conscience told him was wrong.

Religion as he had learned it was a grim business of rules and restrictions. It is noteworthy that one of the avenues by which God came home to his soul at last was the joy of certain poor women of Bedford, talking in the sun, " of the work of God in their souls and how the Lord refreshed them and supported them against the temptations of the Devil by His words and promises." Their happiness was something new to him: " joy in believing " had been no part of his creed. Bunyan at that stage had not learned the truth of Luther's words that " faith is a rejoicing confidence that we have a merciful God." It was these same happy souls who introduced him to Mr. Gifford's church in Bedford, of which he became a member on profession of faith after baptism in the River Ouse.

It would be easy to dismiss Bunyan's religious searchings and self-judgments as too introspective or even pathological. Even stronger words than these have been used. Certainly we ought not to take Bunyan's conscience as a model or to wish others to follow the same path to the knowledge of God. Bunyan himself never supposed that all Christians must follow his experience. Christian indeed trod a like path, but Faithful and Christiana also reached the Celestial City and no such terrors befell them.

But storms are to be expected in the ocean that no one looks for in a mill-pond. The great saints have not un-

commonly engaged in great wrestlings of the spirit that are
not the lot of the ordinary Christian—and perhaps ought
not to be. " It is quite certain," says Macaulay, " that
Bunyan was at eighteen what in any but the most austere
puritanical circles, would have been considered as a young
man of singular gravity and innocence." But Bunyan was
concerned with how he looked in the sight of God, and not
with even puritanical opinion. And as it was not really
the stealing of the pears that troubled Augustine so much
as the motives behind it, so Bunyan was really more
troubled by the sort of person he thought himself to be
than by the things he did, by his sin rather than by his
sins. But his burden, like Christian's, fell from his back
at the Cross of Christ. Salvation was not to be achieved by
the goodness of John Bunyan, but by the mercy of God in
Christ. " That scripture came with great power upon my
spirit. Not by works of righteousness that we have done
but according to His mercy He hath saved us. Now was I
got on high, I saw myself within the arms of grace and
mercy." What he had needed was not another call to
effort and self-help, nor another self-examination, but good
news of divine deliverance for his manacled, impotent and
desperate soul.

Of his decisive enlightenment Bunyan must tell in his
own words in *Grace Abounding*. He had been assailed
suddenly by " a great cloud of darkness, which did so hide
from me the things of God and Christ that I was as if I
had never seen or known them in my life." He felt in his
soul as if his "hands and feet had been tied or bound with
chains." " After I had been in this condition some three
or four days as I was sitting by the fire, I suddenly felt
this word to sound in my heart, I must go to Jesus. At
this my former darkness and atheism fled away, and the
blessed things of heaven were set in my view. While I was
on this sudden thus overtaken with surprise, Wife, said I,
is there ever such a Scripture, I must go to Jesus? She said
she could not tell. Therefore, I stood musing still, to see
if I could remember such a place. I had not sat above two

or three minutes but that came bolting in upon me, ' and to an innumerable company of angels '; and withal the twelfth chapter of Hebrews, about the Mount Sion, was set before mine eyes. (Verse 22.)

" Then with joy I told my wife, Oh now I know, I know! But that night was a good night to me; I have had but few better. I longed for the company of some of God's people, that I might have imparted unto them what God had showed me. Christ was a precious Christ to my soul that night. I could scarce lie in my bed for joy and peace and triumph through Christ."

Not long afterwards Bunyan began to preach, though hesitatingly at first, and showed a singular power of helping other men and women to share his faith in Christ. Under Cromwell's government he was free to preach, but when the Restoration came he was a marked man. Knowing that a warrant had been issued against him and that arrest was inevitable if he persisted, Bunyan refused to withdraw from an engagement to conduct a service. To a suggestion that the service in the little village of Lower Samsell should be cancelled, he replied: " No, by no means; I will not stir, neither will I have the meeting dismissed for this. Come, be of good cheer, let us not be daunted. Our cause is good, we need not be ashamed of it; to preach God's word is so good a work that we shall be well rewarded even if we suffer for it."

Suffer for it he certainly did. That was the beginning of twelve years of imprisonment in Bedford Gaol, for no other crime than that of preaching. His offence was " devilishly and perniciously abstaining from coming to church to hear divine service, and for being a common upholder of several unlawful meetings and conventicles, to the great disturbance and distraction of the good subjects of this kingdom, contrary to the laws of our sovereign lord, the King." The story of those years cannot here be told again. A severe trial to body and soul, his imprisonment yet had certain alleviations, and one was his freedom to write. Several books were written and published. On his release he was chosen as minister of the church in Bedford, and spent three years of liberty in their service. But in 1675 there was a renewal of the reign of intolerance and Bunyan was once more sent to prison, this time for six months. It was then that the *Pilgrim's Progress* was written, or at any rate begun.

As the years passed, Bunyan became a recognized leader among the churches of his neighbourhood; "Bishop Bunyan," they called him, with affectionate playfulness. But he became famous as writer and preacher far beyond the bounds of Bedfordshire. One story tells of how twelve hundred people crowded a church in London to hear him preach at seven o'clock on a winter morning.

Bunyan is among the greatest in English literature. But that was accidental. He was no conscious literary artist, pleased though he obviously was by the fame of his Pilgrim—as his preface to the Second Part charmingly reveals. By God's calling and his own choice he was a preacher of the Gospel by voice and pen. No learned scholar or skilled theologian, as he many times pointed out, John Bunyan yet stands among the greatest leaders of the Church of Christ, and one whose voice has gone out to the ends of the earth. His book has followed the Bible to every land.[1]

It has often been said that *Grace Abounding* has no fellow in Christian literature except the *Confessions* of St. Augustine. It is true, but what a contrast! Ancient Africa and Puritan Elstow; a great scholar steeped in classical culture and a humble brazier with little schooling; an eminent ecclesiastic consulted by the church leaders of the world, and the minister of a proscribed conventicle—but they have the one Lord Jesus Christ.

There is much in Mr. Valiant-for-Truth that reminds one of his creator, and not least his courage and steadfastness. Like Bunyan he found the going hard, but he

[1] The United Society for Christian Literature tell me that they themselves publish editions in 142 languages, and that, of course, is not the whole of the story.

finished his course with triumph. How better could one finish an essay on Bunyan than with that immortal paragraph, great in what it says and great in the telling of it. It cannot be quoted too often.

" After this it was noised abroad that Mr. Valiant-for-Truth was sent for by a summons. . . . When he understood it, he called for his friends and told them of it. Then said he, I am going to my Father's: and though with great difficulty I have got hither, yet now I do not repent me of all the troubles I have been at to arrive where I am. My sword I give to him that shall succeed me in my pilgrimage, and my courage and skill to him that can get it. My marks and scars I carry with me to be a witness for me that I have fought His battles who now will be my rewarder. When the day that he must go hence was come, many accompanied him to the river-side, into which as he went he said, ' Death, where is thy sting? ' And as he went down deeper, he said, ' Grave, where is thy victory? ' So he passed over, and all the trumpets sounded for him on the other side."

VI

A Serious Call

BY WILLIAM LAW (1686-1761)

Two distinguished historians have recorded their judgment that "the first impulse (to the evangelical revival of
the eighteenth century) came from the school of the Non-
Jurors, and especially from William Law's *Serious Call*."[1]
That alone would place the *Serious Call* among the most
influential books in human history, for it would be hard to
exaggerate the significance of the Revival.

At first sight it seems a surprising judgment, for the Non-
Jurors were not evangelicals in any ordinary use of the
word. Certainly Law was never associated with the evangelical party and much of his theology would be very uncongenial to them. He was a high churchman and in later
years a mystic. He admired "the holy solitude" of the
hermit, and made no secret of his regret for the passing of
the monastic system. He advocated celibacy for the clergy,
and indeed makes it plain that he regarded it as the nobler
way of life for all kinds of Christians. And in profounder
questions of sin and salvation he spoke a different language
from the evangelicals. It is an old complaint that there is
too little "Gospel" in the *Serious Call*. "Beyond an in-
tensely earnest conviction of the truth and importance of the
Christian religion, and an honest and consistent endeavour
to lead a Christian life, he really had nothing in common
with either Methodists or Evangelicals."[2]

Yet many facts can be quoted to bear out the judgment
as to his profound influence upon the leaders of that movement. The *Serious Call* was one of the three books that
greatly affected John Wesley at Oxford. Though a serious
rift developed later between John Wesley and Law, which

[1] J. Vernon Bartlet and A. J. Carlyle in *Christianity and History*, p. 545.
[2] J. H. Overton in his preface to an edition of the *Serious Call*, p. xv.

led to the exchange of some unfortunate letters between the two great, but not very conciliatory men, Wesley never ceased to pay cordial tribute to the value of much of Law's teaching, and in particular to his *Christian Perfection* and *Serious Call*. He made the latter a textbook for the highest class in his school at Kingswood and only eighteen months before his death, he described it as "a treatise which will hardly be excelled, if it be equalled, either for beauty of expression or depth of thought." The early Methodists inherited many of their rules of living from Wesley's admiration for it. Charles Wesley said that "the alteration in his views and feelings was produced by reading the *Serious Call.*" Whitefield declared that through it "God worked powerfully upon my soul, as He has since upon many others." Henry Venn tried to frame his life upon its model. Thomas Scott, the evangelical Biblical commentator, whose books greatly influenced William Carey, and whom Newman calls "the writer to whom I owed my soul," dated the beginning of his spiritual life from its reading.[1]

Here perhaps is the place to quote also the striking testimony of Samuel Johnson: "I became a sort of lax talker against religion, for I did not think much against it; and this lasted until I went to Oxford where it would not be suffered. When at Oxford I took up Law's *Serious Call*, expecting to find it a dull book (as such books generally are) and perhaps to laugh at it. But I found Law quite an overmatch for me; and this was the first occasion of my thinking in earnest of religion after I became capable of rational enquiry."[2]

Clearly this must be a remarkable book. But before looking at it more closely, something should be said about its author, though indeed of events, other than the writing of books, there is little to record. Law led a life of quiet retirement, employed in worship and study and in kindliness to

[1] Most of these references, along with a fuller discussion of the question, are to be found in the preface to J. H. Overton's edition of the *Serious Call*.

[2] Boswell's *Life*, Chapter I.

his fellow men. He was born in 1686 at King's Cliffe in Northamptonshire, where his father was a grocer. In 1705 he went to Cambridge, becoming a fellow of Emmanuel and a priest of the Church of England in 1711. At the accession of George I Law refused to take the oath of allegiance and threw in his lot with the Non-Jurors, of whom more in a moment. As a consequence he lost his Fellowship and any prospect of service in the Anglican Church. In a message to his mother he said that concern at the distress his action, with its inevitable effect on his future career, must have caused to her " is the only trouble I have for what I have done. . . . My education had been miserably lost if I had not learnt to fear something worse than misfortune." He became associated with the Gibbon family as a private chaplain and tutor to the father of the famous historian, and remained with them for about ten years. He then retired to his native village where he had been left some small property, and lived there for twenty-three years. In his household were two ladies who shared his views, Miss Hester Gibbon, aunt of the historian, and Mrs. Hutcheson. There they founded between them alms-houses and schools in which they took keen personal interest. These and his well-meaning but indiscriminate charity to all applicants, along with great activity as an author, filled his days. His later books were mystical in character and written under the influence of Jacob Boehme. Wesley characterized Boehme's works as " sublime nonsense," but to Law he was an " illumined instrument of God." With this later mystical phase of Law's thought, we are not here concerned. He died in 1761.

The Non-Jurors, whom Law joined in 1716, were about four hundred Anglican clergy who refused to take the oath of allegiance to William and Mary in 1689. Many of them were outstanding in character and scholarship, including Sancroft, the Archbishop of Canterbury, and seven bishops. They held that James II was still the rightful king. They stood for the independence of the Church from State control in spiritual affairs, though believing in non-resistance.

In spite of their attitude to him King William was unwilling to treat them severely and offered to waive the oath of allegiance if they would agree to discharge their spiritual functions. But the Non-Jurors felt that this implied recognition of the royal supremacy and declined. They were therefore deprived of their benefices. Claiming to be the true Church of England they carried on their ecclesiastical activities in separation, but they never commanded much support among the laity and ultimately died out.

Law certainly had the courage of his convictions, unpopular though many of them were. Our concern here, however, is with the most famous and most influential of his many writings: *A Serious Call to a Devout and Holy Life*, a volume of three hundred closely filled pages.

It owes its power not only to its impressive sincerity and skill in argument, but also to its literary form. Insight into human character is combined with a vigorous and witty style. Serious and even stern in its outlook, it abounds in memorable phrases and humorous characterization. Law could have rivalled his contemporaries Fielding and Richardson as a novelist if his bent had been in that direction. He shows even closer kinship with the essays of Addison and Steele, though his criticism of his fellows is more severe and biting. All this comes out especially in the gallery of portraits by which he drives home his moral. These are plentiful in the *Serious Call*, but he had already used the device to great effect in his earlier work *On Christian Perfection*. There, for example, we meet Philo whose study of "shells, urns, inscriptions and broken pieces of pavement, makes the truths of religion and the concerns of Eternity seem small things in his eyes, fit only for the enquiry of narrow, little and impolite souls." Patronus is "an enemy to Dissenters and loves the Church of England because of the stateliness and beauty of its buildings; he never comes to the sacraments, but will go forty miles to see a fine altar piece." Publius "dies with little or no religion, through a constant fear of Popery." Silvius "laughs at preaching and praying, not because he has any profane principles, but because he happens to be used to nothing but noise and hunting and sports."

Law says he has mentioned such people "to show us that it is not only vices that keep men from the impressions of religion, but that the mere playthings of life, impertinent[1] studies, vain amusements, false satisfactions, idle dispositions, will produce the same effect. A wrong turn of mind, impertinent cares, a succession of the purest trifles, if they take up our thoughts, leave no room for the cares and fears of true piety."

There are many such portraits in the *Serious Call*, most of them admirable in literary skill and effectiveness. Some, it must be confessed, are overdrawn, and some of them deliver long and unconvincing death-bed speeches. Indeed, the whole book is too long. Law is apt to labour his points unduly and he could have said it all more convincingly—at least to a modern reader—in much less space. But there are many memorable pages for which one willingly endures some intervening tedium.

It will be best to let the book speak for itself by quotation, with little comment of criticism or approval. But one more introductory explanation is needed as to its original readers. Perhaps never was Christianity more widely professed in England or church-going more widespread—or more merely conventional. Intellectually Christianity had no serious rivals. The Deists had been routed, with the powerful aid of Law himself. But all the fashionable church-going had little effect upon daily life, or so at least it seemed to Law. What is the use of going to church and paying lip service to Christianity, if you continue to live as you do: that is the constant refrain of the book.

"When the service of the Church is over, they are but like those who seldom or never come there. In their way of life, their manner of spending their time and money, in their cares and fears, in their pleasures and indulgences, in their labours and diversions, they are like the rest of the

[1] A favourite word which Law uses in the old sense of unfitting, not suitable to a man's condition.

world. This makes the loose part of the world generally make a jest of those who are devout."[1] Such Christians are "different from other people, so far as to times and places of prayer, but generally like the rest of the world in all the other parts of their lives. That is adding Christian devotion to a heathen life " (p. 10). " If my religion is only a formal compliance with those modes of worship that are in fashion where I live; if it costs me no pains or trouble; if it lays me under no rules and restraints; if I have no careful thoughts and sober reflections about it, is it not great weakness to think that I am striving to enter in at the strait gate? " (p. 20). He accuses many church-goers of " bended knees, whilst you are clothed with pride; heavenly petitions, whilst you are hoarding up treasures upon earth; holy devotions, whilst you live in the follies of the world; prayers of meekness and charity, whilst your heart is the seat of pride and resentment; hours of prayer, whilst you give up days and years to idle diversions, impertinent visits, and foolish pleasures " (p. 95).

So the main purpose of the books is to call Christians " to live more nearly "—Law would say "exactly "—"as they pray." " It is to excite them to an earnest examination of their lives, to such zeal and care, and concern after Christian perfection, as they use in any matter that has gained their heart and affections." (p. 22.) He sets out to show "that all the parts of our common life, our employments, our talents, and gifts of fortune are all to be made holy and acceptable unto God by a wise and religious use of everything, and by directing our actions and designs to such ends as are suitable to the honour and glory of God " (p. 88).

" For the Son of God did not come from above to add an external form of worship to the several ways of life that are in the world, and so to leave people to live as they did before in such tempers and enjoyments as the spirit of the world approves. But as He came down from heaven, altogether divine and heavenly in His own nature, so it was to call mankind to a divine and heavenly life, to the highest

[1] p. 3. The page references are to Overton's edition. Macmillan, 1898.

change of their whole nature and temper; to be born again
of the Holy Spirit; to walk in the wisdom and light and
love of God; and to be like Him to the utmost of their
power; to renounce all the most plausible ways of the world,
whether of greatness, business, or pleasure; to a mortifica-
tion of all their most agreeable passions; and to live in
such wisdom and purity and holiness as might fit them to
be glorious in the enjoyment of God to all eternity. . . .
This, and this alone, is Christianity, an universal holiness
in every part of life." (p. 99.)

And at the very outset of the book he defines in a
sentence this " devout and holy life " to which he seriously
calls all Christians. " He is the devout man, who lives no
longer to his own will, or the way and spirit of the world,
but to the sole will of God, who considers God in everything, who serves God in everything, who makes all the
parts of his common life, parts of piety, by doing everything in the name of God, and under such rules as are conformable to His glory." (p. 1.)

James Moffatt once remarked that there were Christians
who devoted more serious study to the reduction of their
golf handicaps than they ever gave to the Bible.   So
William Law in his day urged Christians to take their
religion and the development of the spiritual life as
seriously as they took business or even sport. He records a
death-bed speech of Penitens, "a busy notable tradesman
and very prosperous in his dealings," who tells how he had
devoted himself with both enthusiasm and method to his
business affairs, but now realizes with deep regret how
differently he had regarded his religion. " What is the
reason that I have brought none of these tempers to religion? What is the reason that I, who have so often talked
of the necessity of rules and methods, and diligence in
worldly business, have all this while never once thought of
any rules, or methods, or managements, to carry me on in
a life of piety? Do you think anything can astonish and
confound a dying man like this? "

Law also points us to the case of Mundanus, another

prosperous business man, who had made it his pride always to adopt the latest improved methods in his trade. " The only thing which has not fallen under his improvement, nor received any benefit from his judicious mind is his devotion. This is just in the same poor state it was when he was only six years of age, and the old man prays now in that little form of words which his mother used to hear him repeat night and morning." (p.158.)

Law insists that laymen are called to as serious a discipleship as any parson. (And it ought to be added that he does not spare the parsons, or even the bishops, as is perhaps not surprising in a Non-Juror.) " For as all men, and all things in the world, as truly belong unto God, as any places, things, or persons that are devoted to divine service, so all things are to be used, and all persons are to act in their several states and employments for the glory of God." (p. 29.) " A tradesman may justly think that it is agreeable to the will of God for him to sell such things as are innocent and useful in life, such as help both himself and others to a reasonable support, and enable them to assist those that want to be assisted. But if instead of this, he trades only with regard to himself, without any other rule than that of his own temper, if it be his chief end in it to grow rich, that he may live in figure[1] and indulgence, and be able to retire from business to idleness and luxury, his trade, as to him, loses all its innocency and is so far from being an acceptable service to God, that it is only a more plausible course of covetousness, self-love, and ambition." (p. 33f.)

It is interesting to find, by the way, that the " week-end habit " was already there in Law's time. " You see them," he says, " all the week buried in business, unable to think of anything else; and then spending the Sunday in idleness and refreshment, in wandering into the country, in such visits and jovial meetings, as make it often the worst day of the week." (p. 35.)

He has also a good deal to say to the leisured class; " the freedom of their state lays them under a greater necessity

[1] Or as we should say, " in style."

of always choosing and doing, the best things " (p. 43). He urges them to consider the true nature of a Christian gentleman. " They must aspire after such a gentility as they might learn from seeing the blessed Jesus, and show no other spirit of a gentleman but such as they might have got by living with the holy apostles." (p. 98.)

The proper use of money is a large part of the Christian way of life. " If reason and religion govern us in this, then reason and religion hath got great hold of us." (p. 50.) " On all accounts, whether we consider our fortune as a talent, and trust from God, or the great good that it enables us to do, or the great harm it does to ourselves, if idly spent," it is absolutely necessary to consecrate our money to God's service. (p. 53.) He draws pictures of two maiden sisters of independent means, Flavia and Miranda. Flavia " has everything that is in the fashion and is in every place where there is diversion." Her milliner's bills unfortunately prevent her from giving much away, and she is very particular to whom she gives, as most poor people are frauds. " You would think Flavia had the tenderest conscience in the world, if you were to see how scrupulous and apprehensive she is of the guilt and danger of giving amiss." And much more to the same effect.

But Miranda, her sister, " has renounced the world to follow Christ in the exercise of humility, charity, devotion, abstinence, and heavenly affections." She considers her fortune as the gift of God to be " divided betwixt herself and several other poor people and she has only her share of relief from it." " She only differs from them in the blessedness of giving." She has supported poor tradesmen in danger of failing, educated several children picked up in the streets. " As soon as any labourer is confined at home with sickness, she sends him till he recovers twice the value of his wages, that he may have one part to give to his family as usual, and the other to provide things convenient for his sickness." She gives to all who ask : " the merit of persons is to be no rule of our charity." And the rest of the picture fits.

Law has no doubt about it. Miranda's is the only Christian way of using money.

This leads him to devote a chapter to the Christian behaviour of women, a subject to which he devotes not a little space in other parts of the book, including a whole chapter on Female Education. He commends to them Miranda's complete disregard of fashionable dress; clothes should show "the plainness and simplicity of the Gospel." He gives some eight pages to this question. For some women this will be difficult, especially if they are married. Often in Christian history two orders or ranks of Christians have been recognized. For Law the path of perfection leads to "voluntary poverty, virginity, retirement and devotion, living upon bare necessities that some might be relieved by their charities, and all be blessed by their prayers, and benefited by their example" (p. 87). It is because the love of most Christians has waxed cold that men regard him as a setter forth of strange doctrines.

Such a life of complete devotion is in truth one of happiness, and worldliness is silly and tedious; so Law vehemently urges.

The second part of his book is concerned with the practice of prayer. Prayer "is the noblest exercise of the soul, the most exalted use of our best faculties."

Having strongly commended the necessity of early rising for prayer, and the dangers of self-indulgence in wasting time in sleep, Law emphasizes the need of method in planning the times and forms of prayer. "If you are such a proficient in the spirit of devotion that your heart is always ready to pray in its own language, in this case I press no necessity of borrowed forms." But most Christians need to provide against the inconstancy of their hearts "by having at hand such forms of prayer as may best suit us when our hearts are in their best state, and also be most likely to raise and stir them up when they are sunk into dulness." And there is great value in setting apart some definite place for your prayers, to be used for no other purpose. "If any little room (or if that cannot be), if any particular part of a room, was thus used, this kind of consecration of it, as a place holy unto God, would have an effect upon your mind, and dispose you to such tempers as would very much assist your devotion." (p. 152.)

"The first thing that you are to do when you are upon your knees is to shut your eyes, and, with a short silence, let your soul place itself in the presence of God; that is, you are to use this or some other better method to separate yourself from all common thoughts, and make your hearts as sensible as you can of the divine presence. . . . When you begin your petitions, use such various expressions of the attributes of God as may make you most sensible of the greatness and power of the divine nature."

Here is one of the several examples Law gives of how we may fittingly begin our prayers. "O Holy Jesus, Son of the most high God, Thou that wert scourged at a pillar, stretched and nailed upon a cross for the sins of the world, unite me to Thy cross, and fill my soul with Thy holy, humble and suffering spirit. O Fountain of Mercy, Thou that didst save the thief upon the cross, save me from the guilt of a sinful life; Thou that didst cast seven devils out of Mary Magdalene, cast out of my heart all evil thoughts and wicked tempers. O Giver of Life, Thou that didst raise Lazarus from the dead, raise my soul from the death and darkness of sin. Thou that didst give Thine apostles power over unclean spirits, give me power over mine own heart. Thou that didst appear unto Thy disciples when the doors were shut, do Thou appear to me in the secret apartment of my heart. Thou that didst cleanse the lepers, heal the sick, and give sight to the blind, cleanse my heart, heal the disorders of my soul and fill me with heavenly light." (p. 154.)

People of leisure are particularly called to devotion, but the busier people are the more need they have of prayer. "And a little time, regularly and constantly employed to any one use or end, will do great things and produce mighty effects." (p. 157.)

Law commends the value of prayer at regular hours of

the day, at 6 a.m., at 9 a.m., at noon, at 3 p.m., at 6 p.m., and just before bedtime. He sets out a careful plan of appropriate subjects for each hour. It is not possible here to follow his plan in detail, but a few quotations will show the nature of his comments on the different elements in prayer.

In speaking of intercession, he says: "There is nothing that makes us love a man so much as praying for him; and when you can once do this sincerely for any man, you have fitted your soul for the performance of everything that is kind and civil toward him." (p. 257.) " If all people when they feel the first approaches of resentment, envy, or contempt towards others, or if in all little disagreements and misunderstandings whatever they should, instead of indulging their minds with little low reflections, have recourse at such times to a more particular and extraordinary intercession with God for such persons as had raised their envy, resentment, or discontent; this would be a certain way to prevent the growth of all uncharitable tempers." (p. 264.) " For you cannot possibly despise or ridicule that man whom your private prayers recommend to the love and favour of God." (p. 266.)

Here are a few sentences from his chapter on humility. " Humility does not consist in having a worse opinion of ourselves than we deserve, or in abasing ourselves lower than we really are. But as all virtue is founded in truth, so humility is founded in a true and just sense of our weakness, misery, and sin. He that rightly feels and lives in this sense of his condition lives in humility." (p. 183.) " Now as it was the spirit of the world that nailed our blessed Lord to the cross, so every man that has the spirit of Christ, that opposes the world as He did, will certainly be crucified by the world some way or other. For Christianity still lives in the same world that Christ did; and these two will be utter enemies till the kingdom of darkness is entirely at an end." (p. 199.) " And, indeed, the world by professing Christianity, is so far from being a less dangerous enemy than it was before, that it has by its favours destroyed more Chris-

tians than ever it did by the most violent persecution."
(p. 200.)

Here he writes of love. "There is no principle of the
heart that is more acceptable to God than a universal
fervent love to all mankind, wishing and praying for their
happiness, because there is no principle of the heart that
makes us more like God, who is love and goodness itself, and
created all beings for their enjoyment of happiness. The
greatest idea that we can frame of God is when we conceive
Him to be a Being of infinite love and goodness, using an
infinite wisdom and power for the common good and happiness of all His creatures. The highest notion, therefore,
that we can form of man is when we conceive him as like
to God in this respect as he can be, using all his finite
faculties, whether of wisdom, power or prayers, for the
common good of all his fellow-creatures, heartily desiring
they may have all the happiness they are capable of, and as
many benefits and assistances from him as his state and
condition in the world will permit him to give them."
(p. 243.)

"The love therefore of our neighbour is only a branch of
our love to God. For when we love God with all our hearts
and with all our souls and with all our strength, we shall
necessarily love those beings that are so nearly related to
God, that have everything from Him, and are created by
Him to be objects of His own eternal love. If I hate or
despise any one man in the world, I hate something that
God cannot hate, and despise that which He loves." (p. 248.)

These quotations may be enough to give readers who do
not know the book a taste of its quality, and set them on
the search for a copy of it. Certainly those who already
know the *Serious Call* will be glad to be reminded.

It is indeed not a book that one easily forgets. There is
something very impressive about "the uncompromising
simplicity," as the *Dictionary of National Biography* terms
it, with which he sets forth the Christian ideal. Yet there
is something harsh and narrow about the ideal he depicts,
and something grim even in the wit with which he writes.

This austere and ascetic creed is surely not the whole truth about the Christian life. Christianity is not all penance and self-mortification. "Doubtless, as William Law has remarked, a man crossing a river on a tight-rope ought not to be curious about wearing silver slippers, nor will he be much concerned with the colour of the waves. But is that breathless, palpitating figure, poised on a swaying thread twixt earth and heaven, to be taken as the only adequate representation of the Christian life? Are we to hear only of Kedar's tents and the Vale of Baca, and never of the green pastures and the fountains of still waters? Surely not. God hath given us all things richly to enjoy, and whatsoever things are lovely ought ever to engage a Christian's thoughts. It may be that the moral and the imaginative, the evangelical and the artistic aspects of our nature will never fully understand each other. But at least they may fulfil complementary functions, and dwell side by side."[1]

Yet most of us need to ask ourselves if it is concern for the fullness of the Christian life that prompts our criticism of the *Serious Call,* or in part our shrinking from the stern demands that are inherent in the discipleship of Christ. No man who has any desire after the Christian life can read this book without a salutary heart-searching and self-examination. Wesley said it convinced him of "the impossibility of being half a Christian,"—which most of us are content to be. Here is a splendid protest against the apathy and inconsistency of professing Christians.

Froude remarked that he thought the *Serious Call* was a very clever book. Keble retorted that that seemed to him like saying that the Day of Judgment would be a pretty sight. This is a book that judges the reader.

And it is a deeply sincere book. Law meant every word of it and himself lived by the rules he laid down.

He set an example of the charity he commended, and when an anonymous reader of his *Christian Perfection* sent him a gift of £6,000, worth much more in those days than

[1] Coats, *Types of English Piety*, p. 138.

its present equivalent, he devoted it to the building of a girls' school.

Gibbon, the historian, who could be cynical enough about Christians, deeply respected William Law, and he had the fullest opportunity of discovering all his faults. After years of intimacy he tells us that Law enjoyed in his family " the reputation of a worthy and pious man who believed all that he professed and practised all that he enjoined."

VII

An Enquiry

BY WILLIAM CAREY (1761-1834)

"Is William mad?" That was how old Edmund Carey greeted a letter from his son William announcing that he was going to Bengal as a missionary to the Hindus.

It certainly seemed a mad business. William had a wife and three young children—a wife moreover who was very reluctant to leave England. He was engaged in a successful home pastorate. His church at Harvey Lane, Leicester, had had to enlarge the building to accommodate the congregation, and the same thing had happened at Moulton. He was obviously a man with a real call to work at home.

There was no proper organization at his back. After a strenuous struggle over many years he had so quickened the enthusiasm of fourteen young men—nearly all under forty—that they had formed themselves into a missionary society, the only one of its kind in England, with a promised annual income of £13 2s. 6d.¹ Perhaps it amounted to something rather better than that, but certainly no widespread support or enthusiasm was visible. What a time Carey had had pleading with his fellow ministers. One often-repeated story tells how the Reverend Mr. Ryland had reproved his intemperate zeal: "Young man, sit down. When God pleases to convert the heathen, He will do it without your aid or mine." Most of the ministers agreed with his father. Carey was mad.

Even when persuaded in principle that foreign missions were Christian—for the Calvinism of some of them made it hard to admit—they still counselled delay. It was a bad time to be starting a new venture. The spiritual life of many of the churches was at a very low ebb. It was an impossible time to raise money. A long series of wars,

AN

ENQUIRY

INTO THE

OBLIGATIONS OF CHRISTIANS,

TO USE MEANS FOR THE

CONVERSION

OF THE

HEATHENS.

IN WHICH THE

RELIGIOUS STATE OF THE DIFFERENT NATIONS
OF THE WORLD, THE SUCCESS OF FORMER
UNDERTAKINGS, AND THE PRACTICABILITY OF
FURTHER UNDERTAKINGS, ARE CONSIDERED,

BY WILLIAM CAREY.

For there is no Difference between the Jew and the Greek ;
for the same Lord over all, is rich unto all that call upon him.
For whosoever shall call on the name of the Lord shall be saved.
How then shall they call on him, in whom they have not
believed ? and how shall they believe in him of whom they
have not heard ? and how shall they hear without a Preacher ?
and how shall they preach except they be sent ?

PAUL.

LEICESTER:

Printed and sold by ANN IRELAND, and the other Book-
sellers in *Leicester*; J. JOHNSON, St Paul's Church yard;
T. KNOTT, Lombard Street; R. DILLY, in the Poultry,
London; and SMITH, at *Sheffield*.

[Price One Shilling and Six-pence.]

MDCCXCII.

G

culminating in the loss of the American colonies, had impoverished the country. And England was not only poor but restless. Wise men feared that the anarchy of the French Revolution might kindle a flame of rebellion at home. In any case the East India Company had definitely forbidden missionaries to go to India. That ought to settle it.

And after all, who was this William Carey? A humble village pastor without much formal education. His health was such that it is doubtful if any doctor would pass him for the tropics to-day. He was so poor that at times he lacked the very necessaries of life. Even when he became a Baptist minister he had to eke out his pitiful salary with boot-making and school-teaching. He once attended Association meetings with no money to buy lunch and was wandering about the streets when a layman fetched him in and fed him. " Carey's College," as a friend jokingly called it, was his shoe-maker's shop.

A good case could clearly be made out for the proposition that William was mad and could not possibly realize what he was undertaking.

But that was by no means the whole of the story. Even then Carey was in many ways a really learned man and already on the way to becoming one of the foremost linguists of his own or any time. And he was already the author of a little book which the *Encyclopædia Britannica*,[1] looking back after a hundred years and more, declared to mark " a distinct point of departure in the history of Christianity."

One of my treasured possessions is a facsimile reproduction of the original edition of this pamphlet, published in 1792. It is not treasured because it has any particular monetary value: it cost me 2s. (6d. more than the price of the original) and there must be thousands of copies in existence. Rather I treasure it because it helps me to stand in spirit with Carey as he launched this most momentous eighty-eight pages on the world. It is mo-

[1] Eleventh edition. Article " Missions."

mentous as few books have been, even though it was never a best-seller. For it affected for good the lives of millions in many countries, who have never heard of either the pamphlet or its author. It played a most influential part in launching the whole modern missionary movement among all the churches of Protestantism. It certainly shows that Carey had counted the cost and knew where he was going.

I like to look at the title-page (see p. 97), so much more informative than our modern ones.

The pamphlet surprises both by what it contains and by what it omits. One might have expected a fervent appeal based upon a catena of proof texts, drawn indiscriminately from the pages of the Bible; a picture of the dreadful fate of the heathen condemned to hell fire; involved theological argument; attempted eloquence and sentimental outpourings. But it is not like that at all. It is as business-like and matter of fact as a Blue Book, divided into five " sections," one of them an elaborate statistical table, occupying a quarter of the whole. It is logical, factual, eminently practical, like the well-drawn prospectus of a company. " Obligation " is on the title-page and it is the recurring note throughout. Here is an inescapable duty for Christians. The writer has taken immense pains to master his case and he is writing to secure a verdict.

Here is how he begins. "As our blessed Lord has required us to pray that His kingdom may come and His will be done on earth as it is in heaven, it becomes us not only to express our desires of that event by words, but to use every lawful method to spread the knowledge of His name. In order to do this, it is necessary that we should become in some measure acquainted with the religious state of the world; and as this is an object we should be prompted to pursue, not only by the Gospel of our Redeemer, but even by the feelings of humanity, so an inclination to conscientious activity therein would form one of the strongest proofs that we are the subjects of grace, and partakers of that spirit of universal benevolence and genuine philanthropy which appear so eminent in the character of God Himself."

But in fact Christians generally are not alive to this obligation. " Since the apostolic age many . . . attempts to spread the Gospel have been made which have been considerably successful, notwithstanding which a very considerable part of mankind are still involved in all the darkness of heathenism. Some attempts are still making but they are inconsiderable in comparison with what might be done if the whole body of Christians entered heartily into the spirit of the Divine command on this subject. Some think little about it, others are unacquainted with the state of the world, and others love their wealth better than the souls of their fellow creatures. In order that the subject may be taken into more serious consideration, I shall enquire, whether the commission given by our Lord to His disciples be not still binding on us—take a short view of former undertakings—give some account of the present state of the world—consider the practicability of doing something more than is done—and the duty of Christians in general in this matter."

Accordingly Section I enquires " whether the commission given by our Lord to His disciples be not still binding on us." The natural sense and context of the commission excludes any narrow reference to the apostles only. Is there " a natural impossibility of putting it in execution "? " It was not the duty of Paul to preach Christ to the inhabitants of Otaheite, because no such place was then discovered, nor had he any means of coming at them. But none of these things can be alleged by us. . . . Natural impossibility can never be pleaded so long as facts exist to prove the contrary." Roman Catholic missionaries have surmounted the difficulties, so have the Moravians who have " encountered the scorching heat of Abyssinia, and the frozen climes of Greenland and Labrador, their difficult languages and savage manners." English traders for the sake of gain have surmounted all obstacles. " Witness the trade to Persia, the East-Indies, China and Greenland, yea even the accursed Slave Trade on the coasts of Africa. . . ."

"It has been objected that there are multitudes in our own nation and within our immediate spheres of action, who are as ignorant as the South Sea Savages, and that therefore we have work enough at home, without going into other countries. That there are thousands in our own land as far from God as possible, I readily grant, and that this ought to excite us to tenfold diligence in our work, and in attempts to spread divine knowledge amongst them is a certain fact; but that it ought to supersede all attempts to spread the Gospel in foreign parts seems to want proof. Our own countrymen have the means of grace, and may attend on the word preached if they choose it. They have the means of knowing the truth, and faithful ministers are placed in almost every part of the land, whose spheres of action might be much extended if their congregations were but more hearty and active in the cause."

So Carey proceeds to Section II "containing a Short Review of former undertakings for the Conversion of the Heathen." He starts by giving a summary of the *Acts of the Apostles* as an account of the missionary work of the early church, and adds an account of the reputed missionary travels of the apostles to many other parts of the world. He quotes Justin Martyr, Irenaeus and Tertullian as evidence of the spread of Christianity in the first three centuries. He fills pages with references to early missionary work in many parts of the world, giving names and specific places and dates. He refers among many others to the work of Palladius and Columba in Scotland, of Patrick and Finian in Ireland. He tells of the pioneer missionaries to northern Europe: England, Flanders, Westphalia, Saxony, Hungary, Denmark, Sweden, Bohemia, Poland, and other lands. He tells of the missionary work of the Jesuits in the East Indies, China and Japan, of the Spaniards in South America, and the Capuchins in Africa. He records how the work of Wyclif influenced many parts of the

Continent. He speaks of the "amazing increase" of the churches founded by the exiles in America, and of the work of " Mr. Elliot of New England " and " Mr. David Brainerd " among the Indians there. He knows of the work in his own century of Danish and Dutch missions in the East Indies, of the Moravians, and of the efforts of " the late Mr. Wesley "[1] and his ministers in the West Indies.

It is a truly astonishing record of painstaking research, and would have done credit to a professional scholar with access to a great library.

But perhaps Section III is more remarkable still. It contains twenty-three pages of statistical tables in five columns showing: (1) Name of country, (2) length, (3) breadth, (4) number of inhabitants, (5) religion. He lists no fewer than 239 countries, large and small. The detail is astonishing. The Swiss cantons are given separately, and the islands in the Baltic and the Aegean. There are thirty-five entries under Africa, and fifty-five under America. Each little West Indian island has a line to itself: for example, Aruba in the Little Antilles is five miles long, three miles broad and has two hundred inhabitants who are " Dutch, and pagan Negroes." Years of reading and patient note-taking are behind these figures. He had great home-made maps on the walls of his shoe-maker's shop on which he entered every fact he could collect. None of it was guess-work. " I can plod," he once said to a friend!

The conclusion of his calculation is that of the 731 million inhabitants of the world, 420 million were pagan, 13 million Muhammadan and 7 million Jews. There were, he reckoned, 100 million Catholics, 44 million Protestants and 30 million of " the Greek and Armenian churches."

Section IV considers the practicability of something more being done for the conversion of the heathen. Five serious difficulties must be faced: " (1) Their distance from us, (2) their barbarous and savage manner of living, (3) the danger

[1] John Wesley died in March, 1791.

of being killed by them, (4) the difficulty of procuring the necessaries of life, (5) the unintelligibleness of their languages." Distance, he urges, can no longer be pleaded as an obstacle, as witness the fact that ships can now go everywhere and that commerce sends its emissaries to many lands. No doubt they are barbarous, but fortunately that did not deter the missionaries from taking the Gospel to the barbarous Britons, any more than it had deterred Elliot or Brainerd in modern times. "After all, the un-civilized state of the heathen, instead of affording an objec-tion *against* preaching the Gospel to them ought to furnish an argument for it." It is true that whoever goes must take his life in his hands, but we must be prepared for that. And Carey thinks that most of the barbarities practised by the savages were provoked by some real or supposed affront, and were "more properly acts of self defence than proofs of ferocious dispositions." Mission-aries must expect to endure hardship, but if they were prepared to cultivate a plot of ground for their own support and had studied husbandry, fishing and fowling and were provided with the necessary implements, they could main-tain themselves. As to learning the language, he thought that an ordinary man ought to learn "in the space of a year or two, at most, the language of any people upon earth." (Carey had already mastered six languages him-self, with very little assistance!)

The Section closes with a page and a half on the personal qualifications for missionary service. "Let but mission-aries of the above description engage in the work, and we shall see that it is not impracticable."

Section V deals with the practical issue. How is the task to be undertaken? "One of the first and most important" means is "fervent and united prayer." This enterprise will not be accomplished "by might nor by power, nor by the authority of the magistrate, or the eloquence of the orator; but by my Spirit, said the Lord of Hosts."

"We must not be contented however with praying, without *exerting ourselves in the use of means* for the obtaining of those things we pray for." Carey proposes that a society shall be formed "of persons whose hearts are in the work, men of serious religion, and possessing a spirit of perseverance." He wants all Christians to engage in this work, but he directs his appeal especially to his fellow Baptists. "In the present divided state of Christendom" it is more practicable for each denomination to act separately, though in the fullest good will towards each other's efforts.

If everyone helped the money would be forthcoming. The rich can help greatly, those in more moderate circumstances might give a tenth of their income, the poor might give "one penny or more per week, according to their circumstances." Such giving would provide funds for the propagation of the Gospel at home as well as abroad. He suggests that the many Christians who have recently ceased to use West Indian sugar because it is obtained by slave labour, might devote what they have saved in this way to this fund.

Then with one final paragraph of appeal he brings his argument to an end. "What a heaven will it be to see the many myriads of poor heathens, of Britons among the rest, who by their labours have been brought to the knowledge of God. Surely a crown of rejoicing like this is worth aspiring to. Surely it is worth while to lay ourselves out with all our might, in promoting the cause and kingdom of Christ."

The pamphlet was only a means to an end and Carey had set himself to secure action. Chosen as preacher for the meeting of the Baptist Ministers' Association to be held in Nottingham in the spring of 1792 Carey devoted his sermon to the same theme. His text was "Enlarge the place of thy tent, and let them stretch forth the curtains of thine habitations: spare not; lengthen thy cords and strengthen thy stakes, for thou shalt break forth on the right hand and on the left." His message he summed up in two unforgettable phrases: "Expect great things from God. Attempt great things for God."

One who heard the sermon wrote: "It was as if the sluices of his soul were thrown fully open and the flood that had been accumulating for years rushed forth in full volume and irresistible power." Yet deeply moved as they were, the little company of ministers felt that the undertaking was beyond their powers, and they decided that Carey's proposal was impossible. But Carey pleaded passionately with them, and in the end they passed a resolution that " a plan be prepared against the next ministers' meeting for forming a Baptist Society for propagating the Gospel among the Heathens." Perhaps it was largely meant to keep Brother Carey quiet, and to postpone the issue.

The next meeting took place on October 2nd, 1792, in Kettering. The plan does not seem to have been mentioned at the public meeting, but in the evening a group of twelve ministers, a theological student and a layman crowded into a small back parlour. Still there was hesitation. I have already noted some of their objections. The time was most unsuitable for launching a new enterprise. England had been through a series of wars, culminating in the loss of the American colonies. There was much poverty and restlessness. The French Revolution was threatening the stability of society. But Carey's faith and perseverance prevailed and ultimately they came to a unanimous resolve. " Desirous of making an effort for the propagation of the Gospel among the heathen agreeably to what is recommended in brother Carey's late publication on that subject, we whose names appear in the subsequent subscription, do solemnly agree to act in society together for that purpose." They appointed a committee and officers, decided upon the next steps, and promised subscriptions. So with a promised annual income of £13 2s. 6d. they launched the Baptist Missionary Society.

That in itself was a memorable achievement for Carey and his *Enquiry*. For the B.M.S. has now a glorious record of service in many lands during a hundred and fifty years. But in fact Carey's words went far beyond his own denomination.   There is no need to exaggerate or to ignore the fact that other contributory influences were at work.   And *post hoc* is not always *propter hoc*; " after " is not always the same as " because of."

Nevertheless consider this list.

1792   Baptist Missionary Society
1795   London Missionary Society
1796   Edinburgh and Glasgow Missionary Societies
1797   Netherland Missionary Society
1799   Church Missionary Society
1804   British and Foreign Bible Society
1810   American Board of Commissioners for Foreign Missions
1813   Wesleyan Methodist Missionary Society
1814   American Baptist Missionary Union
1815   Basel Evangelical Missionary Society
1822   Paris Society for Evangelical Missions
1824   Committee for Foreign Missions of the General Assembly of the Church of Scotland.

This was not only coincidence of dates. The influence of Carey can be traced upon most of them.   Though the *Enquiry* seems to have been far from a best-seller, it was, to use truly an overworked phrase, epoch-making.[1]

The founding of all these other societies lay in the future, but much thought and prayer and planning clearly lay behind the madness of William's letter to his father.

The perseverance, the tenacity, the vision of the man who was to achieve such great results in India, were all revealed in the young man who had compelled the formation of the Baptist Missionary Society.   How characteristic is the story of the tree he determined to climb as a boy. He tried several times and failed.   He tried again and fell and hurt himself badly.   For some days he was a prisoner at home under his mother's eye.   But when she was not looking he escaped and made straight for the tree and climbed it.

[1] See E. A. Payne, *The Church Awakes*, pp. 33ff. and his article in *International Review of Missions*, April, 1942.

His schoolfellows nicknamed him Columbus—whether because of his adventurous spirit or because of the stories he told them. He devoured the *Pilgrim's Progress,* though he disliked other kinds of religious literature. It was through reading *The Last Voyage of Captain Cook* when he was minister at Moulton that Carey first heard the missionary call and it was to the South Seas that he first wanted to go. This was no sentimental passing enthusiasm. We have seen with what patience he studied his subject, accumulated facts, mastered his argument. In his old age he said that if anyone was going to write his life they would miss the point unless they gave him credit for being a plodder. " I can persevere," he said. Even after he got to India he had to wait seven years for his first convert.

What kind of a missionary did he prove to be?

He was first and foremost an evangelist—not of hell-fire, which he does not mention in his *Enquiry,* but of the love of God. Every department of the varied and far-flung work which he started at Serampore in Bengal is characterized by vigorous and systematic evangelism. His supreme aim was to bring men and women to the knowledge of God in Christ. He had so high a conception of the missionary's calling that when his son received an important government appointment his comment was, " Felix has shrivelled from a missionary into an ambassador."

Christianity as he knew and preached it was a faith that brought full and abundant life. From the first he emphasized the importance of education. He had to support himself in India by his own earnings, as he had always expected, but while an indigo planter in his early years there he founded the first European managed school in North India, the precursor of the whole modern system of elementary education. Gradually he surrounded Serampore with 126 vernacular schools. He opened the first Sunday School in India. He started schools for European children.

Serampore College itself, founded in 1818, is the greatest monument to his genius. To stand in its fine and spacious buildings and to think of what this Christian University has done and is doing in general and theological education, is to have a new idea of the greatness of this " consecrated cobbler," as Sidney Smith dubbed him, not without scorn. It is remarkable that in his first plans for Serampore Carey expounded views as to the use of the vernacular in higher education that were contrary to the opinions of most in those days, but have come to be recognized as the wisest. " We cannot discharge the duty we owe as Christians to India without some plan for combining, in the converts of the new religion, and more especially in its ministers, the highest moral refinements of the Christian character and the highest attainable progress in the pursuits of the mind." It is notable that the Council of fifteen who govern this Christian university has from the first, by Carey's express direction, represented many different churches. It is still to-day an inter-denominational Christian university.

In keeping with this inter-denominational basis for Serampore Carey never missed an opportunity of advocating or practising co-operation with Christians of other churches. He even proposed the calling of a world missionary conference in 1810, a hundred years before it actually took place!

Carey was also a pioneer in the use of literature. He was a great linguist. While still a youth he mastered Latin and then Greek, and he later added Hebrew, Italian, Dutch and French, before leaving England. In India he turned his gifts to good use. Thirty-six translations of the Bible in whole or in part issued from the Serampore Press in his time—not of course all by him. He almost created Bengali as a literary language. Before leaving London he met a young printer called Ward. Carey told him of his intention to translate the Bible into Bengali and urged him to come out in four or five years' time to print it. Ward came and the Serampore Press became the printing centre for the Eastern world of that generation. They published a Chinese Bible. They published Asia's first newspaper, *The Friend of India*.

Carey's linguistic gifts were responsible for his election as Professor in the Government College in Calcutta, founded by the Viceroy.[1] It was a dramatic occasion when the one-time village shoe-maker, at the age of forty-three, addressed the Viceroy and his court in Sanskrit, the ancient classical tongue of India. It is characteristic of the man that in this speech he made explicit reference to his missionary work.

Carey very soon realized the need of grappling with cruel customs and degrading social conditions. At home he had been noted for his vehement opposition to the slave trade. His colleagues said they never heard him pray without a petition for the end of slavery. Much of the credit for the suppression of infant sacrifice in the Ganges is due to him. He had a share in securing the prohibition of *sati*, or the burning alive of widows on their husbands' funeral pyres. The story has often been told of how the edict banning the practice was put into his hands on his way to church with instructions to translate it for publication. He immediately turned back to begin the task, lest a single life should be unnecessarily lost. All forms of ministry to need and suffering had the sympathy of the Serampore group.

From childhood Carey was a great lover of flowers. He wanted to become a gardener, but bad health led him to take up shoe-making instead. This love of flowers he took to India with him. He became a really distinguished botanist and had a remarkable private garden. Even this quality he harnessed to service. He was the founder of the Agricultural and Botanic Society of Bengal and his bust may be seen to-day in the heart of their lovely Gardens. His motive in starting the society was not alone the entirely sufficient one of love of flowers and trees, but also his desire to improve the productiveness and therefore the standard of living of the poverty-stricken Indian peasant.

As one reads the full story of Carey's activities as told

---

[1] It brought him a salary that reached £1,800 a year. Yet Carey died a poor man. All the income of himself and his colleagues went into the funds of the mission. He gave many thousands of pounds to the work.

in the *Life* by Pearce Carey, or that of Deaville Walker, one wonders if there is any missionary method employed to-day that was not practised by this great pioneer.

The breadth and depth of Carey's missionary service is well illustrated in the principles laid down for themselves by the Serampore Brotherhood, to be read three times a year in each station in their charge. Here is a summary.

" 1. To set an infinite value on men's souls.

2. To abstain from whatever deepens India's prejudice against the Gospel.

3. To watch for every chance of doing the people good.

4. To preach Christ crucified as the grand means of conversions.

5. To esteem and treat Indians always as equals.

6. To be instant in the nurture of personal religion.

7. To cultivate the spiritual gifts of the Indian brethren, ever pressing upon them their missionary obligation, since Indians only can win India for Christ."

" Let us give unreservedly to this glorious cause. Let us never think that our time, our gifts, our strength, our families, or even the clothes we wear are our own. Let us for ever shut out the idea of laying up a cowrie (i.e. a farthing) for ourselves or our children. Let us continually watch against a worldly spirit and cultivate a Christian indifference towards every indulgence. Rather let us bear hardness as good soldiers of Jesus Christ." So concludes the Form of Agreement between Carey and his two chief colleagues, Marshman and Ward.

For forty years Carey lived in India without a furlough home, the centre and inspiration of a far-reaching and many-sided work: perhaps the greatest and most versatile missionary of modern times and certainly one of the great names in Christian history. " I esteem such a testimony from such a man a greater honour than the applause of courts and parliaments," was Lord Wellesley's comment as Viceroy on a speech by Carey.

But great, distinguished and widely honoured as he became, he remained a simple, humble Christian. When the young Alexander Duff went to see him at the outset of his own fine missionary career, Carey begged him to speak about Dr. Carey's Saviour and nothing about Dr. Carey.

One of the unforgettable experiences of my life was to stand beside Carey's grave at Serampore and to read on it the only inscription he would allow:

"William Carey. Born August 17, 1761. Died June 9th, 1834.

> A wretched, poor and helpless worm,
> On thy kind arms I fall."

We should not use such language in these days as that quotation from Watts' hymn, but we can appreciate the spirit behind the words. It was true humility. "If God uses me," said Carey once, "none need despair. The God who can do for and through a poor shoe-maker, that which He has done for and through me, can bless and use any."

VIII

The Ring and the Book

BY ROBERT BROWNING (1812-1889)

ONE day in June, 1860, Browning picked out a little square yellow book from among the miscellaneous rubbish on a second-hand stall in Florence. It cost him one lire, eightpence, and contained printed and manuscript material about a once notorious trial, arising out of a sordid case of murder. The book described itself (in Latin which he thus translates) as giving:

> Position of the entire criminal cause
> Of Guido Franceschini, nobleman,
> With certain Four, the cut-throats in his pay
> Tried, all five, and found guilty and put to death
> By heading or hanging as befitted ranks,
> At Rome on February Twenty-Two,
> Since our salvation Sixteen Ninety-Eight:
> Wherein it is disputed if, and when,
> Husbands may kill adulterous wives, yet 'scape
> The customary forfeit.

Later on in London, by some queer chance, he similarly discovered another contemporary pamphlet giving additional facts.

The story fascinated Browning. As Italian jewellers, in making a ring, mixed alloy with the gold, so he mingled his own imaginings with the facts and produced *The Ring and the Book*, his own greatest poem and one of the greatest in English literature. "I fused my live soul and that inert stuff."

Here, in brief, is the story itself. An old middle-class couple in Rome, Pietro and Violante Comparini, managed to marry their young adopted daughter to a noble of fifty, Count Guido Franceschini of Arezzo. Their motive is to

Posizione
Di tutta la Causa Criminale
Contro
Guido Franceschini Nobile
Aretino, e suoi Sicarij Stati
fatti morire in Roma il di 22.
Febb:.io 1698.
Il primo con la decollazione gl'altri
quattro di Forca
Romana Homicidiorum.

Disputatur an et quando Marituf
possit occidere Vxorem
Adulteram
absque incursu pœnæ Ord.rⁱ

(Reduced facsimile of Title-page of Report of the Trial of Guido Franceschini.)

H

obtain an aristocratic alliance and so enter the fashionable world. He hopes for a large dowry, to mend his fallen fortunes. Neither side consults the feelings of the child-wife Pompilia, who is sacrificed to the selfish greed of both parties. Pending the sale of their supposed properties in order to pay the dowry, the parents go to live with their son-in-law at Arezzo. Disappointed at the dull country life, and their treatment in a household where it is scarcely possible to make ends meet, they indignantly return to Rome. The youthful innocent Pompilia has nothing in common with her mean and cruel husband, who vents upon her his rage at discovering that she is not the daughter of her reputed parents and that no money is likely to be forth-coming. After suffering all manner of humiliating experiences, Pompilia determines to join her friends at Rome and is aided in escaping by a young priest, Canon Capon-sacchi. Guido pursues and overtakes them, has them arrested and institutes divorce proceedings. He is met by a counter-suit on the ground of his cruelty. The Court leans to the wife's side. Her flight was judged hasty and compromising, though the charge of infidelity is held un-proved. Merely nominal punishment is meted out; Pom-pilia is sent to a convent for a time and Caponsacchi is temporarily banished to a distant town.

Guido retires to Arezzo, discomfited and angry, to meet the jeers and contempt of his acquaintances. After a few months he hears that his wife has given birth to a son. Moved by ungovernable rage, he determines to wipe out what he pretends to regard as the blot on his good name. He hires assassins, proceeds to Rome and kills Pietro and Violante, and fatally wounds Pompilia, though she lives long enough to give her version of the story and to prove the guilt of her husband. His plea that he was avenging the wrong done to him by his wife's adultery with Capon-sacchi is shown to be false, and it is revealed that he himself had plotted to throw them together in order to win his freedom. He appeals from his judges to the Pope, who reviews the whole case but confirms the sentence of death.

The poem consists of twelve books in which this story is told and retold from the various standpoints of the chief actors and the onlookers. *Half-Rome* sides with Guido. *The Other Half-Rome* takes Pompilia's part. *Tertium Quid*, a superior person, supercilious and cynical, goes over the affair with a fashionable group. So far it has been a versified tale, with little poetry. But then the story takes added force and fire as the Count, Caponsacchi, and Pompilia in turn recount their versions. The leading lawyers on either side rehearse their pleas, in detached, professional spirit. The Pope's searching, sympathetic and profound analysis follows. Then the Count, sentenced and desperate, once more pleads his cause, and an epilogue rounds off the whole.

Soon after the publication of the poem, Carlyle hailed its author with enthusiastic praise, not unmingled with irony: " What a wonderful fellow you are, Browning! You have written a whole series of books about what could be summed up in a newspaper paragraph." That was just Carlyle's little joke, but even the Browning enthusiast may wish the poem shorter. Browning was apt to be long-winded, and for all its genius, *The Ring and the Book* would gain by pruning. Witty as they are, the descriptions of the lawyer's speeches are wearisomely long, and both these books might be passed over by the reader without losing anything essential to the argument. Yet it is an amazing feat to tell the same story ten times over, each time from the standpoint of a different personality, and preserving the individuality of each speaker in vivid and life-like fashion. Each character reveals himself through his own self-expression. And to each monologue the poet's art brings a fitting variety of style suited to the speaker, a cunning adaptation of language and even of rhythm, a choice of such figures of speech as are fitting to the experience and calibre of mind of each.

This method of the dramatic monologue is, of course, one which Browning made peculiarly his own and often employed. He loved to project himself into the soul whose experience he is trying to depict in order to make it tell its own story, and uncover its inner secrets. He sets aside

> The simulation of the painted scene
> Boards, actors, prompters, gaslight and costume
> And takes for nobler stage the soul itself.

He thinks himself into the situation of the soul he depicts, tracing its motives and desires, its weaknesses and foibles as well as its strength of will and honesty of purpose; all the sophistry by which it sought to palliate its evil intentions as well as the good it believed itself to be seeking.

Here, in *The Ring and the Book* we see the tragedy re-enacted, "reconstructed" as the writers of detective stories say, and this is in fact a kind of detective story—from the point of view of the actors in it, and of those who watched from the outskirts. The characters grow as we watch them. Pompilia develops from a child into a woman, as her cruel experience brings out the slumbering qualities of her nature, her innate modesty and sweetness of disposition. Guido changes from a loutish country squire into a man of strenuous action under the stress of his wrongs, real and feigned, and the frustration of his selfish plots; becoming soured, cross-grained, implacably cruel. While Caponsacchi has the latent chivalry of his nature roused by the simple purity of the woman who begs his help; the frivolous priest-ling achieves a strong manhood.

Let us follow the story rather more closely as Browning unfolds it.

After the introductory outline of the story he shows us "One Half Rome" siding with the husband. The Count is more sinned against than sinning. A proud, sensitive man of noble family but fallen fortunes, he had danced attendance for many years upon those who might have given him opportunity for advancement. Tired and hope-less, he determined to retire to Arezzo to end his days in peace and simplicity of life. But his brother Paul counsels

him to marry a wife with money and offers to find him a
suitable match. Designing parents trap him into a marriage
by promises of a rich dowry. But the dowry does not
materialize and he finds himself maintaining the parents as
well as the daughter. Disgusted with the frugal fare and
the dull life the parents return to Rome, full of tales of his
meanness. Once there they declare that Pompilia is not
their daughter at all, but the child of a prostitute whom
they had adopted, and that therefore any promise of dowry
is null and void. The Count tries to make the best of it, but
his young wife carries on intrigues, especially with a hand-
some priest with whom she eventually runs away. Guido
pursues and has them arrested. But the Court lets them
off with a mere show of punishment, holding the charge of
adultery unproven. The wretched Count is goaded by a
counter-charge for divorce on the ground of his cruelty and
then by the birth of a child, falsely alleged to be his.
Naturally he takes the law into his own hands and in a fit
of rage kills father, mother and daughter. If he is to be
condemned for this there is no justice in Rome.

"The Other Half Rome" sides with Pompilia, who has
been throughout the victim of other people's wickedness.
Violante, the mother, was certainly guilty of sharp practice,
but she acted from the best of motives. The Count cared
for nothing but the dowry and treated the parents abomin-
ably. They were half-starved and insulted. Little wonder
they returned to Rome and tried to get their own back.
Guido had then vented his wrath on his luckless child-wife,
who at least was innocent of any crime. He had plotted to
drive her into misconduct to justify divorce. At last she
flees with the help of a friend whom she has scarcely seen,
but who had been described to her as a kindly, resolute
man who would take pity upon her misfortune. The charge
of infidelity is a trumped-up lie. Guido is a low scoundrel
and the world will be well rid of him.

"Tertium Quid," a third party, sits on the fence; it is
hard to tell where the truth lies. Flippant and aristocratic,
he surveys the tragedy with detachment and is sure that a

good deal of the trouble was caused by the Count getting
mixed up with such plebeian folk at all.

> What the superior social section thinks,
> In person of some man of quality
> Who, breathing musk from lacework and brocade,
> His solitaire amid the flow of frill,
> Powdered peruke on nose, and bag at back
> And cane dependent from the ruffled wrist,—
> Harangues in silvery and selected phrase
> 'Neath waxlight in a glorified saloon,
> Courting the approbations of no mob,
> But Eminence this and All Illustrious That,
> Who take snuff softly, range in well-bred ring
> Around the argument.

Next came the three chief personages. Guido and Caponsacchi are addressing the judges, the former after having
been put to question on the rack. Pompilia is talking to a
group round her bed in the convent, where wounded and
dying, she is being cared for.

Under torture, Guido has confessed the murders and is
seeking to set the undeniable fact in the best light he can.
No romantic villain this:

> A beak-nosed, bushy-bearded, black-haired lord,
> Lean, pallid, low of stature yet robust,
> Fifty years old.
> . . . .
> Soft cushioned sits he: yet shifts seat, shirks touch,
> As with a twitchy brow and wincing lip
> And cheek that changes to all kinds of white
> He proffers his defence, in tones subdued
> Near to mock mildness now, . . .
> Now, moved, from pathos at the wrong endured,
> To passion: . . .
> And never once does he detach his eye
> From those ranged there to slay him or to save,
> But does his best man's-service for himself.

Twisting every incident to suit his case, and standing upon
his rights as a husband and head of a noble house, he slurs

over this and emphasizes that, adapting himself to his
audience of ecclesiastics in the most artful and plausible
fashion. He talks piously and with much appeal to senti-
ment, and in the end triumphs in his deed as a vindication
of his honour, and a defence of the sacred institution of
marriage itself.

A very different story is Caponsacchi's, instinct with
suppressed indignation and at times with uncontrollable
eloquence. From the moment when he first set eyes upon
her at the theatre,

> A lady, young, tall, beautiful, strange and sad,

he was solemnized and awed, with a kind of worship that
quickened his frivolous nature to self-sacrifice. He passionately defends Pompilia and himself from any vestige of
unworthy motive. He had spoken to her only once, when
she had appealed to him for help in such a way that he
could not refuse to respond. Throughout he had been
moved only by compassion. Guido, by the intermediary
of a maid, had tried to entrap him into an intrigue with
Pompilia, a subterfuge which he had indignantly rejected.
In flaming language he shrivels up the calumnies of Guido.

In striking contrast to this fiery eloquence come the opening words from Pompilia's death-bed.

> I am just seventeen years and five months old,
> And, if I lived one day more, three full weeks;
> 'Tis writ so in the church's register,
> Lorenzo in Lucina, all my names
> At length, so many names for one poor child,
> —Francesca Camilla Vittoria Angela
> Pompilia Comparini,—laughable!
> Also 'tis writ that I was married there
> Four years ago: and they will add, I hope,
> When they insert my death, a word or two,—
> Omitting all about the mode of death,—
> This, in its place, this which one cares to know
> That I had been a mother of a son
> Exactly two weeks.

Browning presents her " not as a pale, passive victim, but as strong with a vivid, interior life and not more perfect in patience than in her obedience to the higher law which summons her to resistance to evil and championship of the right. Her purity is not the purity of ice, but of fire."[1]   As she lies dying her life with all its pleasures and pains " looks old, fantastic and impossible." Two good gifts remain to her, her baby and the friend who had rescued her.

> Oh, how good God is that my babe was born,
> —Better than born, baptized and hid away
> Before this happened, safe from being hurt!
> That had been sin God could not well forgive:
> He was too young to smile and save himself.
> . . . .
> A whole long fortnight: in a life like mine
> A fortnight filled with bliss is long and much.
> All women are not mothers of a boy,
> Though they live twice the length of my whole life,
> And, as they fancy, happily all the same.
> There I lay, then, all my great fortnight long,
> As if it would continue, broaden out
> Happily more and more, and lead to heaven:
> Christmas before me,—was not that a chance?
> I never realized God's birth before—
> How He grew likest God in being born.
> This time I felt like Mary, had my babe
> Lying a little on my breasts like hers.

With beautiful confidence she " lays away her babe with God," full of trust for his future.

She declares her forgiveness for " that most woeful man, my husband once."

> We shall not meet in this world nor the next.
> But where will God be absent?   In His face
> Is light, but in His shadow healing too:
> Let Guido touch the shadow and be healed!

[1] Dowden, *Browning*, p. 262.

Peace has come at the close of her sad life.

> . . . One cannot judge
> Of what has been the ill or well of life,
> The day that one is dying,—sorrows change
> Into not altogether sorrow-like;
> I do see strangeness but scarce misery,
> Now it is over and no danger more.
> Yes, everybody that leaves life sees all
> Softened and bettered: . . .
> To me at least was never evening yet
> But seemed far beautifuller than its day,
> For past is past.

Her last words are of gratitude for Caponsacchi:

> O lover of my life, O soldier saint,
> No work begun shall ever pause for death!
> . . . My fate
> Will have been hard for even him to bear:
> Let it confirm him in the trust of God,
> Showing how holily he dared the deed!
> So, let him wait God's instant men call years;
> Meantime hold hard by truth and his great soul,
> Do out the duty! Through such souls alone
> God stooping shows sufficient of His light
> For us i' the dark to rise by. And I rise.

The whole picture of Pompilia is unforgettable, a tale, in Swinburne's words, of "piercing and overpowering tenderness."

For present purposes we can pass over the rival lawyers, and turn to the Pope's final verdict; for Guido has appealed to him, pleading "benefit of clergy" on the strength of some minor ecclesiastical office. There are dangers in identifying the views of an author with those he puts into the mouth of a character, yet it is legitimate to see in the Pope's soliloquy not only Browning's own view of the tragedy, but an exposition, though couched in terms proper to the Pope, of much of the author's own Christian philosophy of life. Poetically the finest of all the books, it presents the judgment of a man wise by long experience in all the secrets of the human soul: Innocent the Twelfth,

> Simple, sagacious, mild yet resolute,
> With prudence, probity,—and what beside
> From the other world he feels impress. at times,
> Having attained to four score years and six.

He has been studying the case from early morning and now in the

> Dim
> Droop of a sombre February day,
> In the plain closet where he does such work,
> With, from all Peter's treasury, one stool,
> One table, and one lathen crucifix,

he sums up his findings. Pompilia he pronounces faultless, a rose all the more beautiful because of the dung heap from which it sprang. Caponsacchi is not without blame, but yet a true soldier of Christ courageously daring a difficult task, and nobly resisting the temptations it put in his way. Guido has been doubly wicked, not only in the brutal murder, but in imperilling his wife's soul by placing desperate temptation in her path. For him he can see no excuse and little hope of penitence and salvation. The prospect is all black, but perhaps even here the light of God may penetrate.

> For the main criminal I have no hope
> Except in such a suddenness of fate.
> I stood at Naples once, a night so dark,
> I could have scarce conjectured there was earth
> Anywhere, sky or sea or world at all:
> But the night's black was burst through by a blaze—
> Thunder struck blow on blow, earth groaned and bore,
> Through her whole length of mountain visible:
> There lay the city thick and plain with spires,
> And, like a ghost disshrouded, white the sea.
> So may the truth be flashed out by one blow,
> And Guido see, one instant, and be saved.

Else I avert my face, nor follow him
Into that sad obscure sequestered state
Where God unmakes but to remake the soul
He else made first in vain; which must not be.
Enough, for I may die this very night
And how should I dare die, this man let live?

Reluctantly, yet confident that he is doing his duty, he
signs the warrant for the execution.

Then once more we see Guido, now in the condemned
cell. A Cardinal and a priest are there to tell him of the
sentence and hear his last confession before he goes to the
scaffold. Guido throws off the mask. He is no longer
the suave, cringing devotee of the Church, pleading for his
life. He pours out a wild flood of entreaty, defiance and
blasphemy. The last desperate scream as the officers come
to take him, rises in a startling crescendo of appeal.

> Abate,—Cardinal,—Christ,—Maria,—God. . . .
> Pompilia, will you let them murder me?

Is that the light breaking in the blackness?

For me the writing of Browning has a tonic quality, an
encouraging, inspiring power, and not least in *The Ring
and the Book*. I am thinking of him now as a religious and
moral teacher, rather than as a poet. He has often brought
me great enjoyment because of his mastery of language, the
vivid insight of his descriptions of men and nature, the
sheer beauty of some of his lyrics, his robust humour, his
wit. But he was also, and deliberately, a man with a
message, a Christian message, hard won and firmly held.
Two main themes of this stand out as I think over this
massive poem. One is the worth of the human soul: the
other is God's over-ruling purpose of love.

Browning never thought meanly of human worth and
destiny. Great issues were at stake in every soul. He
called men to courage and effort and urged upon them the
momentous importance of the right decision. There is no

room for neutrality; "life's business being just the terrible
choice." "Side by side with his doctrine that there is no
failure, no wretchedness of corruption that does not conceal
within it a germ of goodness, is his sense of the evil of sin,
of the infinite earnestness of man's moral warfare, and of
the surpassing magnitude of the issues at stake for each
individual soul. So powerful is his interest in man as a
moral agent, that he sees nought else in the world of any
deep concern. 'My stress lay,' he said in his preface to
Sordello, 'on the incidents in the development of a soul:
little else is worth study. I, at least, always thought so.'"[1]

Two passages from the Pope's soliloquy will serve to
illustrate this sense of mighty issues.

> Pompilia wife, and Caponsacchi priest,
> Are brought together as nor priest nor wife
> Should stand, and there is passion in the place,
> Power in the air for evil as for good,
> Promptings from heaven and hell, as if the stars
> Fought in their courses for a fate to be.
> Thus stand the wife and priest, a spectacle,
> I doubt not, to unseen assemblage there.
> No lamp will mark that window for a shrine,
> No tablet signalize the terrace, teach
> New generations which succeed the old
> The pavement of the street is holy ground;
> No bard describe in verse how Christ prevailed
> And Satan fell like lightning!

The other passage is more familiar and frequently
quoted:

> Was the trial sore?
> Temptation sharp? Thank God a second time!
> Why comes temptation but for man to meet
> And master and make crouch beneath his feet
> And so be pedestalled in triumph? Pray
> "Lead us into no such temptations, Lord!"
> Yea, but, O Thou whose servants are the bold,

[1] Henry Jones, *Browning as a Philosophical and Religious Teacher,*
p. 117.

Lead such temptations by the head and hair,
Reluctant dragons, up to who dares fight,
That so he may do battle and have praise.

Browning held that this was no unassisted struggle. God
had made the world as a nursery of souls and He had not
left it. That is the faith expressed by the Pope, not lightly
but in full remembrance of the tragedy he is judging, and
other like tragedies. As he studies nature he sees full
evidence of God's strength and intelligence, and in Christ
he finds evidence that convinces heart and reason that in
Him there is also " love without a limit." This " Christian
tale " reveals to the Pope the true meaning of life.

Beyond the tale, I reach into the dark,
Feel what I cannot see, and still faith stands:
I can believe this dread machinery
Of sin and sorrow, would confound me else,
Devised,—all pain, at most expenditure
Of pain by Who devised pain,—to evolve,
By new machinery in counterpart,
The moral qualities of man—how else?
To make him love in turn and be beloved,
Creative and self-sacrificing too,
And thus eventually God-like.

Those who know little of Browning's thought sometimes
accuse him of a cheap optimism. And they quote, with
sneering commentary,

God's in His heaven,
All's right with the world!

Perhaps on the deepest level this is in fact profoundly true,
but it must be remembered that Browning wrote it as part
of the light-hearted song of a mill-girl on holiday on a
spring morning. And the poem in which it is set reveals
enough and to spare of the sordid realities of ordinary life.
Browning might in fact be charged with giving too much
attention to vice and crime and suffering. Perhaps only

Shakespeare's Iago surpasses his Guido. But if Browning crowds his pages with criminals it is not out of morbidity but because he holds that evil can be transmuted. " His faith in the good seemed to rise with the demands that were made upon it by the misery and wickedness of man, and the apparently purposeless waste of life and its resources."[1] Death does not mark the end of God's work upon the soul. Even for Guido, says the faith of the Pope and of Pompilia alike, as we have seen, there may be hope of remaking; though Caponsacchi seems to picture him as destined for annihilation.

To hold firmly on the one hand to the reality of the moral struggle, and on the other hand to the ultimate victory of the good, to the independence of the human soul and the over-ruling Providence of God, is no easy faith; but Browning will not compromise on either hand. For him, love is God's last but sufficient word.

[1] Jones, *Browning*, p. 111.

INDEX